Bill Russell: The Inspiring Story of One of Basketball's Legendary Centers

An Unauthorized Biography

By: Clayton Geoffreys

Table of Contents

Foreword

Whenever people reflect on the greatest players of all time, it doesn't take long before Bill Russell's name is mentioned. A five-time MVP recipient and twelve-time All-Star, Bill Russell had an illustrious basketball career.

In just thirteen years in the league, he won eleven championships, a feat that puts him tied for the record of most championships won in a North American sports league. Winning was practically in his blood, as even before his successes professionally, he won two college championship titles as well. He is so important in basketball lore that the NBA renamed the MVP trophy after him in 2009.

Bill Russell was so impactful that after his death in 2022, the NBA and NBPA announced that his No. 6 jersey would be retired across the entire league. The game forever changed because of Bill Russell.

Thank you for purchasing *Bill Russell: The Inspiring Story of One of Basketball's Legendary Centers*. In this unauthorized biography, we will learn Bill Russell's incredible life story and impact on the game of basketball. Hope you enjoy and if you do, please do not forget to leave a review!

Also, check out my website at claytongeoffreys.com to join my exclusive list where I let you know about my latest books.

To thank you for your purchase, you can go to my site to download a free copy of *33 Life Lessons: Success Principles, Career Advice & Habits of Successful People*.

In the book, you'll learn from some of the greatest thought leaders of different industries on what it takes to become successful and how to live a great life.

Cheers,

Clayton Geoffreys

Visit me at www.claytongeoffreys.com

Introduction

In the world of basketball or any other competitive sport for that matter, winning is everything. More often than not, fans and history only remember those who have won. The world knows how to celebrate winners by putting them at the apex when it comes to the greatest achievers in the history of basketball. After all, winning a championship is the ultimate goal and the primary purpose of anyone playing the sport.

In its long history, the NBA has seen its share of winners. We have immortalized Michael Jordan as arguably the single greatest player in league history primarily because of his six championships. Players such as Tim Duncan and Kobe Bryant belong in that category as well. And nobody could ever discredit what Magic Johnson and Larry Bird did as individual players and winners, as their respective teams dominated the championship scene in the '80s. However, when it comes to winning, nothing in the history of the NBA is as synonymous with championships as the name *Bill Russell*.

Bill Russell was the single most dominant player in all of basketball as far as winning championships is concerned. With 11 championships under his belt, no other all-time great player has ever come close to his accomplishments as a winner. Yes, even championship greats such as Michael Jordan, Kobe Bryant, Tim Duncan, Kareem Abdul-Jabbar, and Magic Johnson were never even close to what Russell achieved concerning NBA titles.

As the cornerstone of the Boston Celtics in the late '50s up to the '60s, Bill Russell can be considered that team's first true franchise star. While the Celtics had Bob Cousy, it was Bill Russell's toughness as the franchise center that made that team one of the first dynasties in league history. His toughness down in the middle and his nature as a leader were what paved the way for the Boston Celtics' success during those years.

However, unlike most of the greatest players in league history, what defined Bill Russell was that he was *not* the focal point of the team's offense. He was not Wilt Chamberlain, who would power his teams to success by putting up 30 to 50 points on any given night. He was not Michael Jordan, who started and ended plays for the Chicago Bulls. He also was not Magic Johnson, who found open shots for teammates as the primary playmaker. Instead, Russell was the guy that kept the team together.

Standing at a hulking 6'10", which was already gigantic during the '50s and '60s, Russell had the physical capability to dominate his way to high-scoring outputs—but that was not how he led his team to victories. Instead, he did everything else. Russell anchored the paint with his defense to dissuade players from getting to the basket or altering and blocking shots that were within his vicinity. He would stop all-time great centers such as Wilt Chamberlain, Willis Reed, Jerry Lucas, and Bob Pettit from getting easy baskets near the paint. He grabbed rebounds in bunches to secure possessions for his team. And he was also the guy that initiated the famous Boston Celtics' fast-break offense.

When we look at the NBA players that came after Russell, their star power was defined by their ability to score and change the game from an offensive standpoint. As mentioned, Wilt changed the game and introduced new rules to the NBA due to his dominance as an offensive force. Michael Jordan made the NBA more aesthetically pleasing as far as his offensive repertoire was concerned. And Stephen Curry made the three-pointer into the greatest offensive weapon in modern basketball.

But Russell was defined by his ability to do everything else at incredibly high levels. He was known as one of the greatest rebounders of all time and was initiating transition opportunities well before Nikola Jokic, arguably the greatest passing center, was even born. It was his defense that brought him to the dance because Russell was dominating that end of the floor in a way that rivals or even surpasses the defensive prowess of some of the greatest defensive centers in the history of the NBA. As such, regardless of the era that he played in, Russell's ability to defend was decades ahead of its time.

At a time when the defensive rules and lack of seven-footers favored centers and allowed them to easily score 30 points a night, Bill Russell was willing to do everything else except scoring. He was the quintessential leader, and the guy that was willing to sacrifice individual scoring numbers just so the team could win. That very same mentality rubbed off on the Boston Celtics.

With Bill Russell at the helm, the Boston Celtics were unstoppable. His defense initiated the offense when he used his superior size and wingspan to defend the basket. After that, all four of the other Celtics players would run up to the offensive end because Russell was almost always going to secure the rebound. And with the numbers on the Celtics' side, it was easy for Russell to find an open man up the court to throw the ball to and finish their deadly running style of offense.

Bill Russell's unselfishness as a leader was what led to six or more players scoring in double digits for the Celtics every season. It was also what led the team to win a total of 11 championships in the 13 seasons that Bill Russell played for the Boston Celtics. And in two of those championships, he even acted as a playing coach for the team. That all speaks to how great of a winner this giant was during his playing days.

But while Bill Russell was called an unselfish leader, there is a reason why he is still considered one of the all-time great individuals in NBA history. He has won five MVP awards from the '50s to '60s, even though he was up against players like Wilt Chamberlain, Oscar Robertson, Jerry West, and Elgin Baylor, who could all put up ridiculous stats every season. In a way, Russell recreated the definition of a true MVP because he was leading the Celtics to championships and winning seasons despite not having the gaudy offensive stats that his fellow superstars during the 60s were putting up.

Russell was also one of history's premier rebounders, leading the league in rebounding four times and averaging 22.5 rebounds in the 13 seasons he played in the NBA. He is second only to Wilt Chamberlain regarding overall rebounds. After him, nobody even comes close. And though blocks were not yet counted as an official stat back then, there is no arguing that Bill Russell would have ended up at the top of that list had his blocks been credited.

As one of the biggest names in the NBA during his time, Russell was half of what is considered the very first player-to-player rivalry in league history. As almost the polar opposite of Wilt Chamberlain as far as style and personality, Bill Russell had a lot of epic showdowns with the much larger center. And even though Wilt was the most dominant player in the league at that time, Russell is considered the only player that could go toe to toe and even shut him down. The legendary matchups between those two goliaths were the NBA's premier battles of that era.

As a team player, there is no denying how successful a champion Bill Russell was. And as an individual star, he was just as stellar as any of history's greatest players. Combining both aspects of the game creates a player that is synonymous with championships. There is no wondering why he is regarded as the NBA's definition of what it is to be a winner—to the point that the Finals MVP was renamed in his honor.

While we may know Bill Russell as the giant that paved the way for the success of the NBA back in the league's early days, he is also known as a pioneer for African-American players. Russell thrived at a time when racial abuse and disparities were still a primary societal concern in America. He broke barriers by refusing to be treated as a lesser man in his country even after he became arguably the first black superstar in the NBA. He was always active in movements that he thought were beneficial for his fellow African-Americans. And at a time when it was far-fetched to see a black man achieving so much as a player much less a coach, Bill Russell even became the first African-American head coach in league history.

With Bill Russell's contributions, the NBA has become a racially open league that does not devalue people of color and has even expanded across the globe in search of other talented athletes to develop basketball players in different countries. And the same could be said about coaches. Russell demonstrated that your color or race did not matter so long as you could deliver results. Indeed, the league has come a long way from when Bill Russell was still playing and coaching in the NBA. And for his accomplishments in fighting for civil rights, he was even awarded the Presidential Medal of Freedom by Barack Obama in 2011.[i]

You could call him a winner, superstar, pioneer, activist, or legend, but the one word that covers all of those is "great." *Greatness* is what defines Bill Russell the most, and even now, he continues to have an influence on the NBA as a Basketball, FIBA, and College Hall-of-Famer. It is rare to see someone in the history of the sport that can even come close to what Bill

Russell did both as a basketball player and human being. His remarkable story is one of the greatest of our time.

Chapter 1: Childhood and Early Life

It is not uncommon for NBA stars to have a tough early life. However, Bill Russell had a childhood that can be considered tougher than some of the best stars we have today. The future Hall-of-Famer William Felton Russell was born on February 12, 1934, in West Monroe, Louisiana, to parents Charles Russell and Katie Russell.

Growing up in a Southern Louisiana town was not easy for Bill and his parents. Back then, segregation was still very much in practice, especially in the South, and that included West Monroe. The African-American community was separated from the rest of the town and racism was still rampant in society.[ii] The worst part was that Bill Russell was a sickly child that had trouble with illnesses as he was growing up in that segregated town.

Bill has always been open about the troubles he and his family experienced in West Monroe. He said that his father once tried to get served at a local gasoline station only to be put on hold until all white customers were served first. Charles Russell realized that he was put on hold longer than was expected and decided to move elsewhere. But at the moment he wanted to move to another station that would serve him better, he was held at gunpoint and threatened with death if he decided to leave the gas station.[ii]

Bill's mom was not spared, either. At one time, Katie Russell was wearing a beautiful dress outside when a policeman decided to stop her. The policeman had no reason to stop Katie other than the fact that she was wearing that fancy dress. He told her to immediately go home and remove the dress for the unacceptable reason that he thought it was something only a white woman should wear.[iii]

Some would say it was unfortunate, but for the Russells, World War II was sort of a blessing because it was their way out of West Monroe. Because of the war, many black Americans left Louisiana, as they were either needed for service or were required to work to help the country's cause. Charles Russell took this as a chance to escape the harsh racial conditions in Louisiana and went to Oakland, California, where they settled.[ii] Bill was eight years old at the time.

But even after moving to California, Bill and his family still struggled to make ends meet. Poverty became their biggest issue as the Russells jumped from one project home to another. Charles worked low-end jobs as a janitor or worker in a factory because those jobs were what society believed to be fit for black Americans. No matter how hard he worked, the family could not escape poverty. And it only became worse when they suffered one of the biggest losses a family could ever have.[iv]

In 1946, Bill would have to endure the loss of his mother, whom he was especially close to. Katie caught a flu that she could not recover from due to poverty. In the end, Bill suffered an emotional blow that was too hard to bear for a 12-year-old boy, to the point that Charles had to switch jobs so that he could be closer to his son. As his father began to groom him into a better young man all by himself, Bill developed a deep admiration for him and began calling him his childhood hero.[iv]

As Bill tried to move on from his mother's passing, he saw basketball as an escape from the sadness. The young boy spent most of his time playing with his older brother Charlie. The two played the sport with passion and dedication, though Bill had trouble developing his skills because he could not understand the ins and outs of the game.[iv]

Still, it was clear that he was a natural-born athlete. Even as a young boy, he had great physical tools that allowed him to excel in any kind of sport, regardless of whether or not he understood the rules or had great fundamentals. Russell was always a good runner and a high-leaping young man. He also had large hands that allowed him to bridge the gap between himself and other players that had a better grasp of the fundamentals of the sport. But at the end of the day, he just did not have the graceful basics that the other players had. And anyone who saw Russell's playing years in the NBA would know that he was never the most gifted player in terms of his offensive repertoire, and this weakness was probably rooted in his inability to grasp the fundamentals at an early age.

Though Bill was not the most skillful player, he had the physique and instincts to excel in the sport. He ran the floor well for his size and had big hands that could help him catch and handle the ball with ease. He seemed graceful when moving up and down the floor, as he was quickly becoming used to his growing size and frame. However, skills and race were still the biggest reasons why he was cut from the basketball team when he was in junior high. But that did not stop him from eventually becoming the basketball legend he is today.

Chapter 2: High School Career

Bill Russell attended McClymonds High School in West Oakland for his prep years. When he got to high school, he almost did not make the team once again because of his lack of fundamental skills. That was always his weakness as a youth. No matter how passionately he played the sport, Russell still struggled to play basketball the right way.

Because Bill could not keep up with the rest of the players regarding those skills, he was almost cut from his high school team when he was still a freshman. But his high school coach saw something in him that no other person saw. Coach George Powles saw that Bill Russell had potential because of his size and athleticism.[iv] He might not have been as good as the other players as far as those skills, but his innate coordination and athletic prowess made him worthy of consideration.

The first thing that Powles thought was that Russell could be a dangerous basketball player if he could work on his fundamentals. Any coach would know that fundamentals can be taught but physical gifts can never be coached. Russell had the physical gifts and athleticism of a true athlete. Powles thought that he could teach the young man to work on his skills so that he could become an unstoppable player. But the challenge was not whether or not Russell was willing to work on his fundamentals. Instead, Powles needed to overcome the issue of *race*. It was not going to be easy to tell Russell what he needed to do to improve as a player because he was white and Russell was black.

It was not easy for Powles to approach Bill. After all, the young Russell did not have the best experience with white authority figures in the past. The same could be said about his parents, who both experienced their share of racial discrimination in the past even after moving to California from Louisiana. This made Bill a difficult young man to mentor for *any* coach, let alone a white one.

In truth, no one could blame Russell, or any black young man during that era, for getting quite apprehensive or anxious whenever there was a white authority figure telling them what to do. And the Russell family were never strangers to racial discrimination. Ever the assertive man, Bill was not going to let someone tell him what he needed to do just because this person was white. And while Powles' role was to coach the young man to become a better player, it still was a challenge for him to allow Russell to understand that the color of their skin had nothing to do with their coach-and-player relationship.

Ultimately, George Powles was able to overcome that racial barrier and left a lasting positive impression on Bill. When the young man was about to get cut, Powles gave him a chance to redeem himself because he saw the makings of a great basketball player in him. Powles encouraged Russell never to quit playing basketball and to focus on his fundamental skills. He was a raw prospect that had the athletic ability and size of a skilled player but lacked the necessary training that allowed most other players to excel in the sport. But Powles believed that Russell was going to perform great if he could improve on the basics.[iv]

For Bill, this was such an excellent experience. As a young black boy growing up at a time when society and even the law still did not treat African-Americans as equals, Russell met a coach that was willing to give him a chance because he saw something in him. He even regarded his experience with Powles as being similar to a warm welcome.

That is one of the best things about basketball and sports in general. Society finds a way to segregate and discriminate against people in all sorts of ways, such as race, color, and gender. We may have come a long way, however, even to this day, incidents continue to occur that prove our battles against discrimination are far from over. But in basketball, the best coaches and players only care whether you have the talent to play the sport or not. It hardly matters whether you are black or white as long as you can play.

In today's modern generation, basketball players are often judged by coaches and scouts based on their combination of skills and athleticism. It is no longer relevant what color the player is because what really matters is whether the player has the skill set and physical tools to become successful. And Powles was one of the rare high school coaches during the 1950s to see that skin color had nothing to do with whether or not Bill Russell could become a dominant player in the future.

Knowing that he had the trust and belief of his coach, Bill began to work harder on his game so that his skills could keep up with his size and athleticism. And luckily for him, he went through a growth spurt. He began to grow bigger than most teenagers at a time when guys over 6'6" were playing center and power forward. However, Russell was still a third-string player back then and was still in the middle of his growth spurt.

When Bill was still growing as far as skills and height, he met George Mikan. At the time, the legendary Minneapolis Lakers center was the best and most dominant force in the NBA. Mikan stood 6'10" and was taller, stronger, and bigger than any of the centers that he went up against. It was like he was the Shaquille O'Neal of the '40s and '50s because nobody could stop him. All the other big men of that era were the size of shooting guards and small forwards in today's modern basketball. As such, Mikan was the giant that all the other power forwards and centers looked up to while they were learning the game of basketball as young men.

When Russell met Mikan, he was a growing 6'6" center for McClymonds, and far from the best player on his team. However, Mikan saw potential in the future Hall-of-Famer and decided to talk basketball with the young teenager for 15 minutes or so. It was an unforgettable experience for Bill, who never thought that a third-string center like him was worthy of the attention of basketball's greatest player at that time.[v] Russell started looking at Mikan as one of his childhood heroes after meeting the Laker giant for the first time.

After that fateful encounter, Russell was determined to get to where Mikan was as a player. He began to work harder until his extra effort paid off. And with Russell's improvement and growth in both skill and size, he soon started dominating the high school basketball scene in Northern California. He was also the state's most dominant prep player after he led McClymonds High School to championships. No other high school player at that time had the combination of skill and size that Bill Russell had. Still, it was his defense that made him stand out as one of the greatest high school players the country had ever seen.

While Bill could perform well on the offensive end from time to time thanks to his superior size and athleticism, he truly distinguished himself on the defensive part of the game. The big man from McClymonds was a defensive force to be reckoned with that dominated the game better than any other player could. He was not always the most consistent offensive player, but his defense was what set him apart and allowed his team to win back-to-back state championships.

Bill Russell was a trailblazer and pioneer for his style of defense. At a time when players were far from being as athletic as the ones we have seen in the last three decades, it was rare for defenders to leave their feet when protecting the basket. The norm back then was to stay on your feet or to stay flat-footed under the rim so that you could quickly react to any plays.

However, Bill Russell played it differently. He did not stick to the norm. Instead, he left the ground and used his long arms and athleticism to block or change shots near the basket. At first, coaches were quick to try to correct Russell's style of defense, but when they saw how effective it was, they eventually allowed him to defend the way he wanted to.

"To play good defense ... it was told back then that you had to stay flatfooted at all times to react quickly," Russell said. "When I started to jump to make defensive plays and to block shots, I was initially corrected, but I stuck with it, and it paid off."[vi]

While some coaches today would still prefer players to stay on the ground with their arms raised when protecting the basket, the best defenders have a knack for knowing the right time to leave their feet to go for blocks or defensive plays. In that sense, Bill Russell was ahead of his time in the '50s because he already instinctively knew when it was the best time to leave his team to defend the basket. He was like the Dikembe Mutombo of his era because of how well he timed his jumps to block shots.

Of course, Russell's knack of knowing when it was best to try to block or contest shots was not merely a gift or product of genetics. He got to that point primarily because he worked hard off the court and as a student of the game. In an autobiography, Russell admitted that he was obsessed with studying his opponents' tendencies. He was reading scouting reports as a part of his pre-game preparation so that he could understand his opponents' style of play and know how to defend them most effectively. His preparation was so in-depth that he even studied their footwork to know which foot they moved first or jumped with so that he could time his movements and jumps accordingly. In that sense, Russell's ability to defend the basket came about as a result of his endless study and dedication to his craft.[vii]

Russell was also using Dell Magazines' publications during the 50s to understand the habits of the opposing best player on the teams that they played against. He was a clever scout that could figure out the moves of the opposing players by using whatever resource was available to him at that time. And he often used a mirror to practice how to defend the go-to moves of the opposing players.

Unlike today's generation, which has the luxury of using social media and smartphones to scout their opponents and understand the details behind their best moves, Russell played things out in his mind while reading magazines and other scouting reports on his opponents. The mirror was his best friend when it came to imagining how his defensive assignment was going to attack him.

So, if he had the endless resources that are available to today's generation, Russell would have likely been even more dangerous as a defensive player. This goes to show just how far he was willing to go when it came to his defensive assignment. Even in high school, he went the extra mile just to understand how to stop opposing players.

Though Bill Russell was making an impact on both ends of the floor for McClymonds, racism was still a significant factor in why very few colleges were willing to take the young African-American high school star. College recruiters did not even try to recruit him until the University of San Francisco's Hal DeJulio saw the young center play for the first time.

DeJulio witnessed first-hand what Russell could do on the floor. He described him as a player that was still miles away from the rest of the pack as far as fundamentals were concerned. Indeed, Russell was not yet a good scorer in high school but more or less a mediocre one that went for a big night once in a while. But DeJulio was impressed by how Russell was seemingly ahead of his time regarding basketball IQ and feel for the game. It seemed as though he knew what he was doing, especially in clutch situations.[iv] His skills may not have been up to par with his defensive mindset and advanced understanding of the game, but Russell already had a basketball IQ that was elite, especially when it came to how well he saw the floor and how he was able to see what the offense was doing.

The University of San Francisco offered the young giant from McClymonds a college scholarship, which was something Bill Russell's family could not afford in any other situation. Knowing that playing college basketball was going to be his escape from poverty and the racist circumstances he always found himself in, Bill accepted the offer wholeheartedly and believed that moment to be the most significant turning point in his life.

Chapter 3: College Career

When Bill Russell joined the University of San Francisco, he decided that he would make the best out of his college basketball career because it was his best and probably only chance at a life away from poverty and racism along with all of the negative things that society threw at him. Playing for the freshman team, his sole focus was improving his fundamentals and developing into a player that was far from the "atrocious" offensive player Hal DeJulio described him to be in high school.

The moment Bill was eligible to play for the San Francisco Dons in his sophomore year in college, he immediately made his impact known. Russell became the starting center for the team and went on to show his brilliance as a rare basketball talent. He was the perfect fit for what was a half-court and defense-oriented squad led by coach Phil Woolpert.

Bill Russell's greatness on defense, as well as his ability to score when he was given a good opportunity to do so, was exactly what the Dons needed that season. And being a person of color, he was also a pioneering icon who led many fans of the sport to believe that black people could perform just as well and perhaps even better than most other white Americans at that time. He was even part of the first three black players to ever start at the same time in a college basketball game. One of the other two players was K.C. Jones, who would go on to be a future teammate of Russell's in the NBA.

At about 6'10", Bill Russell had grown to his mature height but was still a lanky and skinny player compared to many other shorter centers in the country. However, his build and frame gave him an advantage. Instead of trying to contain players one-on-one using strength and heft, Russell excelled at playing help defense. Using his basketball IQ, he kept track of where the ball was at all times and also watched his opponents moving without the ball. And when the ball found its way near the basket, Russell was always there to protect it by quickly rotating over to help out.

Woolpert's coaching style was perfect for Russell. On offense, he was allowed to slow the pace down and play a half-court style that enabled him to pass the ball around to players that were better suited to score. Meanwhile, on defense, he was allowed to play the same roaming defense that a lot of shot-blocking big men in the NBA today play.

Russell often had to guard smaller forwards on defense because Woolpert would rather put his bulkier and stronger players on centers. While the bulkier players were trying their best to contain opposing centers using their strength, Russell could play help defense whenever he was needed. He blocked shots as a help defender that could leave his man for a split second before covering up for his teammates. And whenever the offense went to the forwards that Russell guarded, he used his length to block their shots and swat the ball away aggressively.

With his length, guard-like quickness, and cat-like reflexes, Bill Russell was the ultimate defensive center and was ahead of his time. It was like putting a quick and athletic big man like Anthony Davis back in the '50s to defend the basket against smaller and less athletic players. In that sense, Russell was simply owning the paint as a defender and was the centerpiece of a defense-oriented San Francisco team. He was blocking shots left and right while making sure that every rebound fell right into his huge hands. And even if he was not blocking shots, he was making a difference in the paint just by altering shots or scaring away smaller players that were wary of his presence.[iv]

The University of San Francisco Dons made it all the way to the Western Regionals that season before losing to USC in the title game. It was a surprisingly good year for USF because critics did not believe they could become as good as they were that season—and it was primarily because of how dominant Bill Russell was at the center position. The big man averaged 19.9 points and 19.2 rebounds in his first season for USF.

So, just how good was Russell during that season? Well, the NCAA typically changes its rules in response to how unfair some players seem to be because of their dominance on the court. Some examples of this include the institution of the goal-tending rule in 1945 because of how George Mikan was blocking shots that were already near or at the basket, as well as the prohibition of the dunk in 1967 because of how unstoppable Lew Alcindor (now Kareem Abdul-Jabbar) was when he was near the basket.

In Bill Russell's case, the NCAA widened the lane coming into the 1954-55 season because he was simply too overly dominant as a defender near the basket. Officials in the NCAA thought that widening the lane would prevent Russell from camping near the basket long enough on the defensive end to make a difference. But that did not matter because he was still an incredibly gifted defensive specialist that could block shots regardless of what the rules were.

Sports Illustrated once wrote, "If Russell ever learns to hit the basket, they're going to have to rewrite the rules."[iv] That was how incredible of a defensive talent he was. As such, the NCAA had to change its rules to make sure that Russell was not going to make the games unfair for the opposing teams. Still, there was no taking away the fact that he was far more than just a physical specimen that could block shots because of his height, length, and athleticism. After all, it often takes more than just physical tools to become a

21

great defender in the game of basketball. In Russell's case, he had the IQ and on-court presence that allowed him to dominate the defensive end regardless of whether or not he had the physical tools of a great defender.

But everything else was not all sunshine and roses for Bill Russell. Although he joined the USF Dons to escape racism, it was still difficult for him and some of his black teammates to avoid poor treatment. They were often the butt of jokes during games, and even their own USF fans hurled racist jeers at them at times. However, those were not the worst because Russell had learned to ignore the jeers from the crowd.

During the 1954 All-College Tournament held in Oklahoma City, Russell and his black teammates were not even allowed to enter the hotels in the city. Because of that, the entire team decided to stay in a college dorm during the length of the tournament since they thought that nobody should be left behind while the others were allowed to stay in hotel rooms. To this day, Bill Russell continues to regard that experience as one of the best bonding moments he and his teammates shared. And instead of putting himself down, he allowed himself to become a better and more hardened man because of those experiences.[viii]

With Russell's resolve hardened and his skills improved, he led USF to one of the finest seasons the school has ever had. After taking the All-College Tournament crown in Oklahoma City despite the inhospitable welcome from the town, the University of San Francisco went on to dominate the rest of the country on their way to capture the national championship. And in the middle of it all, both figuratively and literally, was Bill Russell's dominant play on both ends of the floor.

Even though he was still considered a raw offensive player as far as his scoring skills were concerned, he was putting up points at a career pace and even set what was then an individual scoring mark of 39 points in one of the early games of the season. But it was still his defense that helped pace the entire team's play that season, as Russell was controlling his matchups whether they were smaller or bigger than he was.

And speaking of bigger, it was unusual during those days for any player to be bigger than the already big 6'10" Bill Russell. Players back then were not built as tall and massive as the ones we see these days. We rarely saw seven-foot behemoths during the '50s. That said, Russell's height and length were crucial for him on the defensive end, especially when he was matched up with smaller players.

But coming into one of their games in the NCAA Tournament, Russell had to match up against a much taller player. What was worse was that he was just recovering from a severe cold that kept him out in the majority of the second half of their last game. With the odds stacked against him, Russell was seemingly at a disadvantage when the Dons were on their way to take on Oregon State.

Oregon State had the pleasure of fielding one of the tallest men in the entire country. It was rare for anyone to stand over seven feet tall back then, but they had a 7'3" giant of a man patrolling the paint for them. Swede Halbrook was his name, and he was averaging over 20 points and more than 14 rebounds that season. In fact, he was so dominant for Oregon State that UCLA head coach and one of the most legendary figures in all of basketball, John Wooden, said that there was no way that Bill Russell would win that matchup, even though he thought that the young USF center was the best defensive player he had ever seen in his life. And to make things even worse, Oregon State had *another* seven-footer in Phil Shadoin to throw at Russell.[ix]

While Bill Russell did not dominate the much bigger Halbrook on the defensive end, he was able to hold his own and neutralized the giant to help his team escape with a dramatic victory. It was one of the best games in NCAA history, as several accounts say that 6'1" guard K.C. Jones was able to outjump Halbrook in a jump-ball situation late in the game. After that dramatic one-point win over Oregon State, the University of San Francisco Dons dominated their way against Colorado to secure a date with La Salle in the NCAA Finals.

Even though Russell was steadily making a case and a name for himself as one of the premier basketball players in the entire country, there was a consensus belief that he was not the best. Writers, analysts, and coaches believed that La Salle's Tom Gola was the greatest college player ever and arguably one of the best players in the world at that time. That was because he could do extraordinary things for his team with or without the ball in his hands. Gola was one of the pioneer, all-around great players of basketball.

But while the championship game was billed as a battle between Russell and Gola, it was K.C. Jones who came up big on both ends of the floor for USF. He defended Gola remarkably while making sure he was scoring well for his team. This led people to believe that the Dons were more than just Bill Russell's team but were, in fact, a group of unselfish players that were willing to step up and make plays at any given time.

The Dons crushed La Salle to win the national title for the very first time, and Bill Russell went on to say that he was "greater than the greatest."[viii] In response to that, he was given the NCAA Tournament's Most Valuable

Player Award and became the first African-American player to be named MVP. He was named first team All-American. In addition to that, Russell averaged 21.4 points and 20.5 rebounds the entire season for the national champions.

Though Russell had already distinguished himself as the best player in the country after winning the title, he thought that race was still an issue. There was a belief that nobody could accept a black man as the best player in college basketball even though Russell had the numbers and accomplishments to back it up. That said, even after everything he won that season, the Northern California Player of the Year Award went to another center not named Bill Russell. It was at that moment that Bill realized that individual accomplishments were mere consolation prizes compared to team achievements.[x]

"At that time it was never acceptable that a black player was the best. That did not happen," Russell said. "My junior year in college, I had what I thought was the one of the best college seasons ever. We won 28 out of 29 games. We won the National Championship. I was the MVP at the Final Four. I was first team All-American. I averaged over 20 points and over 20 rebounds, and I was the only guy in college blocking shots. So, after the season was over, they had a Northern California banquet, and they picked another center as Player of the Year in Northern California. Well, that let me know that if I were to accept these as the final judges of my career I would die a bitter old man."

Still, not getting recognized as the best player in Northern California did not bother Russell's focus. He was always an unselfish player that made sure his team was in the best position to win, regardless of whether or not he was the one putting up points on the board.

Because Russell's mind was set on putting the team before himself, the USF Dons were once again heavy favorites coming into the 1955-56 season and were considered the number-one team in the nation, especially because they had the best player in all of college basketball. They started the season continuing the ridiculous winning streak they had started the previous season and were seemingly unstoppable.

However, no matter how dominant Bill Russell and the USF Dons were, the most discriminating basketball fans still had not seen what the 6'10" giant could do. New York was (and still is) one of the biggest basketball markets worldwide, and its people are some of the most spoiled fans when it comes to watching the best players in the world.

New York fans had seen it all. They'd seen the giant George Mikan do his thing in his prime. They'd also watched Boston Celtics greats such as Ed Macauley and Bob Cousy perform in front of them. These fans knew real talent when they saw it and were impressed by the offensive talents of all the basketball greats they had seen. But somehow, they had not seen Bill Russell. At that time, Russell was widely regarded as the best player in all of college basketball. Some would even say that he was better than anyone playing professional basketball! However, New Yorkers had yet to witness Russell and what he could do.

The University of San Francisco Dons went to New York for that season's Holiday Festival Tournament. With that, the arena was packed and the people of the Big Apple were excited to see how great of a player Bill Russell truly was.[xi] Was he the next George Mikan, who dominated teams on the offensive end with his size? Was he really better than Tom Gola like he said he was? Or did he have the ball wizardry that Cousy had?

At first, New Yorkers were confused. Here was a massive 6'10" giant that struggled to score from the post when he had the ball near the basket. He was every bit of the physical specimen that Mikan was and was even longer and more athletic. However, he did not seem to have the refined offensive skillset that the great Laker possessed. But even if he was not as offensively gifted as George Mikan, was Bill Russell a good shooter, or was he a rare ball wizard at his size?

It was *neither*. The fact was, Russell could not shoot the ball from the standard 15-foot line. Whenever he got the ball at the free-throw line, he was hesitant to shoot it and was more likely to look for another teammate. It was as if he was looking lazy on the offense, and was reluctant to receive a pass or even shoot the ball even though he was open. And even when he decided to shoot the ball, Bill Russell was clanking his jumpers.[x] He could not even dribble the ball very well to attack the basket.

With what they were watching, those New Yorkers were wondering if he truly was the greatest college basketball player that ever existed at that time. Silence filled the air as Bill Russell failed to dazzle and impress the crowd with his scoring gifts or lack thereof. At that point, it was clear that this giant of a man was not a scorer. But if not that, what could Russell do that warranted a national title and the mantle of best player in the world?

Fans were beginning to see that Bill Russell was an unspectacular offensive player, but the senior from USF was slowly and steadily showing people that basketball was played on *both* ends. The longer the tournament went on, the more Russell proved he had skills on one end that no other player in the history of the sport has ever had.

At a height of about 6'10", Russell was usually bigger and longer than most of the players on the court. He may not have used that size to score but he was effective in areas that other players often struggled at. Russell was utilizing his height, length, large hands, and athleticism to soar over all the other players to grab rebounds as if his hands had magnets to attract the basketball. In fact, he soared so high that he set a school record for the high jump and was considered the seventh-best in that sport for the year 1956. That said, going up for a rebound was like taking candy from a baby for Bill.

But that was not what finally got the people of New York roaring for him. This was a 6'10" giant of a man who could deny his man the basketball on one part of the floor but could suddenly take two quick strides to block a shot from an opposing player that was seemingly open before Russell came to deny him a basket. For a man of his size, his quickness and reaction time were top-notch.

Bill Russell was simply an overpowering presence on the court. He may not have been hitting jumpers or scoring from the post, but he was doing everything he could to help his team win. The man was picking up his teammates' misses and jamming baskets down with authority. He was making sure that his opponents did not have a second chance at a basket by sucking up all the rebounds. He made sure that nobody had a good look at the basket with his ability to swat shots or psychologically affect his opponents' decision to shoot. Sure, he was not George Mikan on offense, but he did not need to be. He did everything else better than the Laker legend.

One of Russell's defining moments during that tournament was when USF met Holy Cross in the semi-finals. Holy Cross had Russell's future Boston Celtics teammate Tom Heinsohn, a 6'7" forward that could put up 27 points and 21 rebounds at any given moment. But Russell, despite not averaging the gaudy numbers that his future teammate typically did, made sure that he was the better player by limiting Heinsohn to only 12 points. A well-known inside scorer himself, Heinsohn could not do anything against Russell and was forced to shoot jumpers instead of attacking the basket.[x] Russell finished that game with 24 points and 22 boards as USF eventually came up with the victory and went on to win the tournament.

After the tournament, Bill Russell was named the Most Outstanding Player. The whole affair turned out to be a Bill Russell show, as the best player in the entire nation was given an opportunity to showcase what he could do on the court. He turned doubters into believers as the University of San Francisco eventually won the NCAA Championship for a second straight season in 1956. He averaged 20.6 points and 21 rebounds in his senior year while getting numerous Player of the Year honors that season.

As Russell's college career with the University of San Francisco was coming to a close, playing for the professional ranks was quickly becoming a reality for the nation's best player. The first team that was interested in his services was the Harlem Globetrotters. However, the team owner only wanted to speak with Russell's college coach, Phil Woolpert, and not Bill himself.

When Woolpert met with Abe Saperstein of the Globetrotters, Russell believed that the team owner thought he was too smart to be talking to him directly. Instead, it was the team's assistant coach that entertained Russell with jokes while Saperstein met with Woolpert. Due to the behavior of the Globetrotters' owner, Russell thought that it was best for him to take his talents straight to the NBA instead of playing for a man that did not even want to talk to him. Believing it to be racial prejudice, Bill Russell declined the Globetrotters' offer and declared for the NBA draft.[iv]

With Bill Russell leaving the collegiate ranks, a new giant was quickly becoming the nation's most sensational college player. A young freshman named Wilt Chamberlain was turning heads with his domination even while playing for Kansas' freshman team. Wilt was taller, stronger, bigger, and more athletic than Bill Russell.

Sadly, the two giants never got a chance to meet in the collegiate ranks because Russell was on his way out when Chamberlain was playing for the freshman team. Fans could only imagine what would have happened if Bill and Wilt met back in college. Of course, Chamberlain was always the better physical specimen, but Russell had a better understanding of the game. Russell was also a bit older and more experienced compared to the younger giant. As such, there might have been a chance that Russell could have made things tough for Chamberlain if they had been opponents in college.

The NBA, however, is an altogether different story. Russell's epic battles with Chamberlain have since become the stuff of legends and could dwarf even Godzilla's battle with King Kong. Wilt was eventually going to become the greatest college basketball player in history at that time, just a few years after Bill owned that title. Some fans quickly forgot what Russell could do after seeing what Chamberlain did. But for now, Bill Russell was on his way to fulfill his dream of playing in the NBA to escape racism and live a life where he never had to worry about whether he could provide for his family or not.

Chapter 4: NBA Career

Getting Drafted

After such a spectacular college career in San Francisco, Bill Russell was undoubtedly the best player in the entire collegiate ranks. Some would even say that he might have already been better than the best that the NBA could offer. However, he had yet to prove that and was still on his way to make a mark in the NBA by joining the draft.

Anyone who had the top overall pick would go for Russell ten times out of ten. After all, he was a proven winner in college and had the tools that could translate to the NBA to make him a productive contributing player at the very least. However, the consensus belief among NBA teams was that he was going to be the next big thing in the league.

Physically, Russell was at the top of his class. Rarely did you see seven-foot players back then, but Russell was close to that mark at 6'10". And what was even more impressive was his wingspan. The big center from San Francisco was coming into the draft with a remarkable 7'4" wingspan that helped make him a hawking presence in the middle.

Players that stood close to seven feet tall back then and had wingspans that were several inches longer than their height were rare. Granted, there were giants in the NBA at the time, but most of them did not have the athletic gifts and mobility that someone like Russell had. As such, Russell was a generational talent in terms of his physical abilities because his athleticism and mobility could rival what most of the athletic NBA players that even today's generation are capable of.

When it came to his athletic gifts, Bill was also in a class of his own. He was a great runner that could run 440 yards in less than 50 seconds. He even set records in the high jump and was considered one of the best in the entire world in that sport, even though he never competed in the Olympics. With that said, Russell was also not the bumbling giant that many men his size are. If you compare his physical tools and athletic gifts to a recent player, Russell was a lot like Anthony Davis in the sense that he could cover ground quickly like a guard but could defend the paint well with his incredible wingspan and vertical leaping ability.

Back in college, Davis was dominating everyone else because he had gifts that not a lot of players had. He had the mobility of a guard, the length of a true center, and the jumping ability of a forward. As such, he dominated the NCAA on his way to a national championship in just his freshman year in college. Those were the very same things that Russell did when he was in college. The only difference was that they were separated by more than five decades. But the fact that Russell was capable of the things that Davis was doing in college in 2012 suggests that Bill would have also been a defensive beast in today's modern generation.

Bill Russell used his size and athleticism to defend the basket like no one in the history of the league has ever done before. Using size, he could body up and defend opposing centers and forwards one-on-one with relative ease. At one point in the 1955 NCAA Tournament, he was even defending two seven-footers at the same time. But Bill Russell's specialty as a defender was not one-on-one defense, even though he excelled at that. Instead, he was an even better help defender.

Because of his guard-like quickness and reflexes, Russell had the ability to cover ground in a heartbeat. If he was matching up with a center on the left block, he could immediately recover to the right side of the basket to contest or block a seemingly open shot from another player. In a sense, it was like he made denying shots near the basket his personal art form. He knew when it was time for him to leave his defensive assignment to cover up his teammates' defensive lapses and swat away shots that opposing players thought were going to be uncontested or open.

Speaking of blocks, Bill Russell was a pioneer in that regard. The basketball world had seen its share of giants, but blocking shots was not something they did regularly, and that was because the big men of the past were not as athletic as Bill Russell was. That said, coaches would rather have them defend the basket by staying on their feet to make sure they could react more quickly. Nobody wanted their centers jumping up to try to block shots.

It made sense for centers to stay on their feet to block or contest shots because, at that time, some centers were simply tall enough to alter or swat away shots. Of course, staying on the ground meant that a defensive player had enough time to recover in case the opposing player passed the ball to a man near the basket. That would have allowed the center to recover in time to protect the basket at the last minute. Russell, of course, changed the game.

Bill Russell was different. He had the length and athleticism that allowed him to jump off the ground to try to block or contest shots. At the same time, he jumped quickly enough to recover in case of a shot fake or drop pass at the very last second. Russell was simply a different breed of rim protector, as he could do things that no other player before him was capable of.

As they often say, a defensive play does not end until your team secures the rebound. In that regard, Russell was still the best in the world. On top of making sure the opposing team missed their shot attempts, Russell used his size, length, and athleticism to grab rebounds. The ball just always found its way into his huge baseball-mitten-like hands. Nobody in the world could rebound like Russell could. He always made sure to finish defensive stops by securing the rebounds.

But for all his talents as a defender and rebounder, Russell was not a complete basketball player. Ever since his youth, he always had subpar basketball fundamentals. He did not dribble the ball very well and could not shoot jumpers that many players could make with their eyes closed. He was not the best post player either because he was usually hesitant to score the ball one-on-one when he was near the basket. Russell was, at best, an opportunistic scorer that got his points by being at the right place at the right time to receive drop passes or jam the ball back after getting an offensive rebound.

Still, Russell was not someone that a coach would name the focal point of the team's offense. Instead, most of the other players on the team were allowed to generate offense. While Russell was the team's leading scorer during his senior year in San Francisco, he just did not have the post presence that other big men had. And that was always his biggest weakness as a player.

Even though he was not the polished offensive player that would have given teams trouble because of his size and athleticism, Bill Russell was doing everything else better than the rest of the world. He defended the basket as if his life depended on it and rebounded the ball like a black hole sucking up everything in sight. There was no one better than him in the 1956 draft, or probably all of the drafts that came before that year.

Before the draft, Boston Celtics' head coach Red Auerbach was already eyeing Russell because he believed him to be the missing piece that could give his team their first-ever NBA championship.[i] Red wanted Russell because of his defense which, at that time, was odd because centers were mostly utilized for their ability to score and rebound rather than defend. But because Auerbach already had high-scoring guard Bob Cousy and Bill Sharman, and had already drafted gifted forward Tom Heinsohn with their territorial pick, what he thought the Celtics needed was a defensive centerpiece.

In basketball, there is only so much that the offense can do to cover the team's lack of defense. It might be true that the goal is to score more points than the opposing team. But if the team does not prevent the opponents from scoring, a loss is all but guaranteed. That was why, for all of Bob Cousy's talents as the point guard that changed the position, the Boston Celtics could not win a championship. In 1956, the Celtics led the league in points scored but were dead last in points allowed. That was when it was clear that the team needed someone that could guard the basket and make life easier for the guards and forwards. Bill Russell was the man that Auerbach thought was going to fill that role for the Celtics.

The problem that Red Auerbach had to overcome, however, was that they were not in the position to draft Russell because the league awards higher draft picks to lower-seeded teams. Because the Celtics finished second during the 1955-56 regular season, they had no chance of drafting Russell with their draft. What made it even worse for them was that they had already given up their first-round draft pick for the territorial draft they used to acquire Tom Heinsohn.

Red Auerbach's moves during the 1956 offseason were a testament to his genius. He put in motion a series of moves that would eventually shake the very foundations of the NBA on his way to building the league's most dominant dynasty. The rest of the NBA had no idea what was eventually going to happen, as only Auerbach had the foresight to know that he was on his way to building a dominant team.

Auerbach first tried to persuade the Rochester Royals, who had the top overall pick, to not draft Bill Russell. The Royals were looking for a skilled guard and were not willing to pay Russell's signing bonus. Knowing that, and also knowing that basketball was not the most lucrative sport back then, Red offered to give the Royals the much more lucrative Ice Capades show for one week if they did not draft Russell. The Rochester Royals accepted and drafted Sihugo Green instead. The Royals also said that they were not financially capable of paying the $25,000 signing bonus that Russell was requesting. As such, their best bet was to draft Green, whom they thought would be great to pair with Maurice Stokes, a strong rebounder himself.

But Red was not done. The Boston Celtics still needed to secure the second overall pick. To that end, Auerbach gave up long-time All-Star center Ed Macauley and Cliff Hagan to the St. Louis Hawks in exchange for the second overall pick. While the Celtics may have given up one of their top stars and a young player who was yet to play for them because of military service, Auerbach was certain that drafting Bill Russell was worth all the sacrifices.

With the second overall pick in the hands of the Boston Celtics, Auerbach went on to draft Bill Russell. Later in the draft, they also drafted Russell's San Francisco teammate, K.C. Jones. With that brilliant maneuvering, the Celtics acquired three franchise cornerstones after drafting Heinsohn, Russell, and Jones all in the same class. Those same players would all be vital for building what would eventually become a Celtics dynasty.

But before Russell could join the Boston Celtics, he had to serve his country in the Olympics first. He was named the captain of the US basketball team of the 1956 Olympics in Melbourne, Australia. Though he could have opted to skip playing for his country to start playing for the Celtics for a full season right away, he wanted to represent his country.

Russell led the US team to victory to become one of the few players to win the NCAA championship and an Olympic gold medal all in a single year. That done, he was set to join the Boston Celtics in the middle of the 1956-57 season to give them a chance to win a title.

Rookie Season, First NBA Championship

Russell joined the Boston Celtics late in December of 1956 when the season was already well underway. And just as Red Auerbach had hoped, Russell showed every indication that he would become the missing piece that could push the Celtics to become title contenders. The center played his first game on December 22nd of that year and finished with 6 points and 16 rebounds in about 21 minutes of action. It was an underwhelming debut, but Russell did enough to give the Celtics the win over the St. Louis Hawks in that game.

Nevertheless, it took a few games for Russell to fully adjust to his new team's system and his new teammates. He even shot 7 out of 31 from the field through his first three games. However, on December 26th, he showed his true form after going for 15 points and 34 rebounds in a win over the Philadelphia Warriors. That was the first of what was to become many double-double games for him.

On December 30th, Russell would have another dominant output for the Boston Celtics. In a win over the Syracuse Nationals, he went for 20 points and 32 rebounds. Then, on January 6, 1956, he had another monstrous 30-rebound game by going for 31 boards and 18 points in a win over the Fort Wayne Pistons. After the shaky three-game start, it was clear that Russell had already grown accustomed to his team, as he averaged 15 points and 26.5 rebounds in the next six games.

Though he was not known for his offensive skills, Russell went for a new career high of 25 points on January 18th against the Hawks. He also added 20 rebounds to his name in that win. A week later, he had another good scoring output by going for 24 points on top of 28 rebounds in a win over the Minneapolis Lakers. Bill would break his career high by going for 30 points twice later in the season.

On February 5th, Russell went for a new career high in rebounds. In that win over the Syracuse Nationals, he had 19 points and 34 huge boards. Even as a rookie, Russell was rebounding and defending better than what was expected of him. He was, in fact, the best rebounder in the entire league at that time.

As the dust of the regular season settled, the Boston Celtics had won 44 games. Bill Russell was undoubtedly every bit the defensive force he was advertised to be after going for 14.7 points and a league-leading 19.6 rebounds that season while playing 35.3 minutes on average. However, he would not win Rookie of the Year since he had only joined the team in December. The award would go to his teammate, Tom Heinsohn, who himself had a spectacular rookie season as well.

With Russell in the fold, Red Auerbach's plans had been put into motion. The legendary head coach wanted the Boston Celtics to play a fast-paced style of game that was predicated on Bob Cousy's ability to run the floor hard and set up his teammates for the best shots possible. That was why the Celtics did not have one player that dominated scoring possessions.

However, the problem in the previous seasons was that they did not have a defensive force that could rely on, not only to make sure nobody scored on them but also to secure the rebounds. But because of Bill Russell, the Celtics now had a fallback option on defense. The rest of the Celtics were confident to press hard while playing defense because they knew that Russell was behind them protecting the basket. The common phrase "Hey, Bill" became their top defensive play, as Celtics players would simply call out Bill Russell's name if they wanted him to help them out on defense.[iv] Using his quickness and long strides, Bill could easily help out and double on defense and then recover back to his man if the ball happened to find his original defensive assignment.

In a sense, it was Bill Russell's defense that started the Boston Celtics' offense. His ability to block shots near the basket made it possible for his teammates to have enough confidence to play aggressively and gamble on defense because they knew that Russell was always going to be near the rim in case their aggressive play or gambles did not pay off.

Having Russell protecting the paint also allowed the Celtics to masterfully implement the team's pressing defense. His athleticism allowed him to get back on defense quickly enough to cover the paint, while the guards and forwards applied pressure on the opposing team's ball handlers. Before Russell's arrival, the Celtics could not apply this defense to perfection because one of the weaknesses of the pressure defense was that the lane would be open if the ball handler could break the press. But because Russell could cover up the weaknesses of all the other players on the defensive end,

39

the guards and wings could pressure the ball handlers without worrying too much about whether or not there was someone in the paint. Meanwhile, the opposing offense was wary of Russell's presence in the paint. This led to mistakes on the part of the opposing team's ball handlers whenever they got too close to the basket.

When their aggressiveness and pressing defense worked to cause turnovers, the Celtics were quick to run the break and score on the other end. And if they could not force turnovers, Russell was always going to be there to block or contest shots and then grab rebounds. The other four guys would often run the floor hard on offense as soon as Bill completed the defensive play because they knew that their big man would always get the rebound. In a sense, having Russell was a win-win situation for the Celtics' aggressive style of defense.

The fact that Russell was also great at covering defensive lapses as a help defender was what prompted the "Hey, Bill" defense. The moment an opposing offensive player had a chance to get a step on his man, the defender would simply say "Hey, Bill" to prompt the gigantic center to come and swat the shot or, at the very least, scare away the opposing player.

There were also times when a Celtics player would use this defense to request a double team from Russell. But because Russell was so quick to get back on defense, he could still cover the man that he left whenever the ball got to that open player. It was such a luxury for the Boston Celtics to have him as their top defensive gem because Russell had the IQ and physical tools to perfect the art of playing help defense.

Russell was such a great defender that he was already being called an unfair advantage by different people all over the league. The Philadelphia Warriors'

Eddie Gottlieb once protested that Russell was a one-man zone defense. At that time, zone defenses were not allowed in the NBA. But Gottlieb said that Russell was basically playing zone while all the other players on his team played man-to-man. Moreover, he also said that the Celtics center goal-tended a lot of shots without getting called for any of them.[xii]

A player that is often called "unfair" by any opponent is certainly one that stands head and shoulders above the rest of the pack. That meant that Russell was quickly changing the game, as he was basically telling the entire NBA to step it up so that they could get to his level or, at the very least, adjust the way they were doing things to make sure that his defensive abilities were neutralized. And the true mark of a generational talent is the ability to change the game or force other teams to evolve.

That season, the Boston Celtics improved from being the sixth-worst team on defense to the top defensive team in the league. They also led the entire NBA in rebounds. And as anyone might have guessed, it was all thanks to how Bill Russell was dedicated to doing all the important things other than scoring. Yes, one man can make so much difference even though basketball is a team sport. And the presence of this one man changed the entire course of the Celtics' franchise as it transformed them into a world-class organization that had a winning mentality.

But the mission that season was still incomplete. The goal was to win a championship, and Russell placed the Celtics in an excellent position to do so.

Boston would meet Syracuse in the Eastern Division Finals, which was Russell's first taste of the NBA playoffs. He did not disappoint in his first playoff game by going for 16 points, 31 rebounds, and 7 blocks. Russell was so good in that series that he frustrated opposing big man Dolph Schayes and limited the star power forward's production. The Celtics went on to sweep the Nationals in that series. After two consecutive national titles in college and an Olympic gold medal, Russell was playing for a championship yet again.

The championship series was not going to be an easy finals for Bill Russell because he was given the difficult task of trying to limit St. Louis Hawks' star player Bob Pettit, who was one of the best scorers and rebounders the NBA had to offer at that time. That task was so difficult that Russell allowed Pettit to score 37 points in Game 1 as the Hawks went on to win that one in double-overtime.

In Game 2, however, Russell was a defining piece in helping his team win by 20 points by going for 25 big rebounds. He also helped limit Pettit to only 11 points on 3 out of 16 shooting. But the Hall-of-Fame big man bounced back big to make sure Russell was not going to limit him in the entire series. The Hawks fought the Celtics hard to force the series to seven games.

When everyone thought Game 7 was going to be a battle between Russell and Pettit, it was Heinsohn who picked up the scoring and kept Boston alive in the most crucial game the Celtics played at that point in time. Heinsohn was battling with Pettit on the scoring end and put up 37 points while Russell tried his best to make sure the opposing big man was not getting his points so easily. But while it was Heinsohn who kept the Celtics competitive because of his scoring, Russell's defense was the primary factor that eventually sealed the championship win for the team.

The Celtics were up 103 to 102 with about 40 seconds left on the clock. After a rebound by St. Louis, Hawks player Jack Coleman received an outlet pass near midcourt and proceeded to try to lay it all the way in since there were no Celtics players to impede or defend him. And because Russell was battling for the rebound, he was far behind Coleman and was probably somewhere near or under the opposing team's basket. That said, there clearly was no player near Coleman to try to prevent him from scoring. But Bill Russell did not give up.

Coleman may have had a significant running start when he caught the outlet pass at midcourt and may have only needed a few seconds to reach the Celtics' basket to try to score the ball, but Russell was making his way back to try to defend that shot. It was no secret that Russell was a great runner, having competed as a track-and-field star in college. And in that incredible defensive play, Bill used every bit of what his long athletic legs could give him to save his team's chances at a championship.

The moment the 6'7" Coleman crossed the top of the key, he started gathering the ball up for a layup. However, he did not know that Russell had already caught up to him and was there blocking the ball from behind as it slammed the backboard hard.

Yes, Russell came all the way from the other baseline in the blink of an eye and performed a thrilling chase-down block decades before LeBron James was even born. Bob Cousy, a strong runner himself, called that play "the most incredible physical act I ever saw on a basketball court." Bill Russell's famous block on Jack Coleman is now widely known as the "Coleman Play."[xiii]

Chase-down blocks have become a norm in today's NBA, but the defender is usually only about ten feet behind before catching up to prevent the player from scoring. The chase-down block was also made into LeBron James' signature defensive play. As a 6'9" player that could jump out of the building

43

and run the floor hard, James could easily catch up to a player in transition and swat the ball when the player thought he had a layup or a dunk. We saw James do that in the 2016 NBA Finals to help seal a championship win for the Cleveland Cavaliers.

But to put Russell's block into perspective, he was almost half a court away from Coleman when he began sprinting back on defense. He also did that from a dead spot or stationary position, while Jack Coleman was already accelerating from his running start. That said, one can only imagine how fast Bill Russell was running just so he could reach the play in time. He was like a bolt of lightning streaking down the court.

This play from Russell was also a testament to how wide the gap was between him and the other players in terms of athleticism. While players of that era were already athletic compared to the average man, they were not as athletic as the incredible athletes that we see in today's NBA. But Russell's athleticism was well ahead of its time, as he showcased a level of athleticism that we could only see in today's modern basketball era. The fact that he was far more athletic than most players of his era was also one of the qualities that made Russell an elite defensive player that transcended eras.

Sparked by Bill Russell's massive defensive play, the Boston Celtics had enough energy and fight left in them to win the game in double-overtime. The franchise had just won the first of what was to become many NBA titles. But as they say, the first one is always the sweetest. And for the rookie Bill Russell, it was all in a day's work for the man that had won two NCAA titles, an Olympic gold medal, and an NBA championship in only a span of two years and a few months.

First MVP Season, the Calm Before the Dynasty

After winning the NBA championship in just his rookie year, Russell was on top of the world. The entire Celtics organization felt the same, of course, and they were considered the team to beat entering the 1957-58 season. Boston kept their core players while the young duo of Russell and Heinsohn were getting better with experience, training, and chemistry.

Because Russell was already clearly the Boston Celtics' centerpiece on the defensive end and was the man responsible for initiating the fast-break offense, he got more minutes and was allowed to own the rebounds while the other players were out there streaking to wait for outlet passes. This allowed Boston to win 14 consecutive games to start the season.

In the middle of that 14-game run, Bill Russell had fantastic performances, but there was one that stood out. On November 16th, Russell had one of the best games in the history of the league against the Philadelphia Warriors. He owned his role as a rebounder and went on to collect a new record of 49 rebounds. By doing so, Bill eclipsed Neil Johnston's 39-rebound record by 10 boards. He also collected a still-standing NBA record of 32 rebounds in a single half. Russell also added 28 rebounds in that win over the Warriors.

Throughout the season, it was normal for Russell to collect 20 or more rebounds. There were even a lot of instances where he had more than 30 boards. However, on February 12, 1958, he set another record and went for 41 massive rebounds in a win over the Syracuse Nationals. At that time, that was the second-best rebounding game in the history of the league. Then, 11 days later, he collected 38 rebounds in a win over the Warriors. By doing so, Bill Russell owned three of the top four rebounding games in the NBA at that time.

Because of Russell's dominance in the middle as a defender and rebounder, the Boston Celtics went on to easily clinch the Eastern Division's top spot and were once again the best defensive team in the entire NBA. Due to his accomplishments as a leader and the anchor of the NBA's finest team, Bill Russell was voted as the league MVP for the first time in his career. He averaged 16.6 points and 22.7 rebounds. That was the very first time in league history that any player averaged more than 20 rebounds in a single season.

At that time, there were people in the media that wondered how and why Russell was named the MVP. After all, the media voted him into the All-NBA Second Team, and that means that he was not the favorite center among the members of the press. This was when it became clear what being the "most valuable" player meant in the NBA.

The argument was that Russell was simply much more valuable to his team than any other player in the league was to their respective teams. It might be true that there were other players who were better scorers and passers than Russell, but no one could argue against Russell's value to the Celtics as the team's best defender and rebounder.

Of course, the players had a say in what it meant to be valuable to a team. It was not until 1980 that members of the media were given a say on who deserved to be the MVP. Before that time, the right to vote on who deserved to be the MVP belonged to the players exclusively. Because the players saw what Russell did to their teams whenever they played the Boston Celtics, they knew how valuable he was. Only a player that had the experience to face Russell's defense knew just how much he changed the outcome of a game just by covering the paint and making up for his team's defensive lapses. As such, the players in the league knew that Bill Russell deserved the MVP.

With their MVP manning the paint, the Boston Celtics were so dominant that they ran through the Philadelphia Warriors in the Eastern Division Finals and beat them in five games. At the same time, Russell proved his mastery over the Warriors and averaged 15.6 points and 28.8 rebounds in the five games he played against Philadelphia. With Russell and the Celtics playing that way, that team from Boston seemed like the favorites to win the championship all over again.

Facing the St. Louis Hawks in a rematch of the 1957 Finals, Russell and the Boston Celtics went into Game 3 with the series tied. However, the center went on to miss the remainder of Game 3 after going down with a foot injury in the middle of the bout. Russell missed Games 4 and 5 as the Celtics went into Game 6 with a 3-2 series deficit.

Russell returned in Game 6 but it was clear that he was not the same dominant giant he normally was. He played only 20 minutes in that game and was visibly hobbled. He was not the usual giant that could easily snatch rebounds with his incredible athletic gifts. Bill also struggled to defend the paint and was not the imposing presence that everyone knew him to be. It was evident that his foot was still bothering him but he still wanted to play to help give his team a chance to stay alive.

But with Russell unable to play his usual imposing self in the middle, Bob Pettit made mincemeat out of the Celtics giant's diminished defensive capabilities. The St. Louis Hawks' legendary big man went on to score 50 points as the Celtics were felled in six games. Nobody knew what might have happened had Russell been healthy for the entire series. There were those that claimed the Celtics would have won that series had Russell been healthy. Auerbach dismissed such claims by saying, "You can always look for excuses ... We just got beat." But Bill Russell would never lose another NBA Finals.

The Dawn of a Dynasty, Wilt Chamberlain's Arrival, Dominating the NBA Championship

After getting hampered by a foot injury in the 1958 NBA Finals, Russell was on a mission to redeem himself during the 1958-59 season. He was visibly healthy and unhindered by his previous injury and went on to have another dominating season, not only for himself but also for the Boston Celtics, who were getting better every season.

Russell proved himself every bit the dominant force in the middle for the Boston Celtics all season long. The man in the paint for the Celtics was putting up numbers befitting of the league's premier paint defender and rebounder. And the best part about it was that he was carrying the Celtics all season long with his monstrous efforts on rebounding the ball and defending the basket.

On December 12, 1958, Russell had only the third 40-rebound game in league history at that time. In that win over the Cincinnati Royals, he went for 20 points and 40 rebounds. With that performance, Russell had become the owner of the top three single-game rebounding performances in the NBA. Simply put, there was no rebound he could not snatch up with his long arms and huge hands.

While Bill Russell was not really known as a scoring center, he did have flashes of brilliance in that aspect of the game as well. He tied his then-career high 32 points twice that season. And in one of those games, he even had a great performance on both ends after finishing with a 30-30. On Christmas Day of 1958, he had 32 points and 33 rebounds in a win over the Knicks in front of the rowdy New York fans.

With Russell putting up numbers matching or close to those in virtually every game, there was no way the Boston Celtics were going to get beaten that season. Russell remained consistent and averaged 16.7 points and 23 rebounds. Once again, he led the league in rebounding and upped his previous career-high average in that department. And the best part of it all was that Russell led the Celtics to a then-league record of 52 wins in a single season.

But for some reason, Bill did not win MVP honors. That award went to Bob Pettit, who was his rival at that time. Pettit led the league in scoring and was able to regain his status as the best-scoring big man in the NBA. Meanwhile, Russell was still the best defensive player in the league and was undoubtedly the one person that changed the entire culture of the Celtics.

Russell led the Boston Celtics to a seven-game series win against the Syracuse Nationals in the Eastern Division Finals. It was a competitive series where both teams traded wins on their home floors. The Celtics were lucky enough to have home-court advantage against the Nationals. In those seven games, Russell averaged 19.1 points and 26.7 rebounds.

While the Eastern Finals may have been difficult, Russell and his Celtics found the Minneapolis Lakers easier opponents in the NBA Finals. The Lakers had rookie superstar Elgin Baylor, but Russell was more than enough to stop him from scoring. The Celtics eventually defeated the Lakers in four games in what was the first incarnation of many Finals battles that the two future rival teams would have. In that series, Bill Russell averaged 9.3 points and 29.5 rebounds.

With that sweep over the Lakers, Bill Russell and the Celtics were now winners of the NBA Championship for the second time in three years. That win also solidified Russell's place as arguably the finest player the NBA had to offer. In fact, he was so dominant on the defensive end in that series that Lakers' head coach John Kundla even said that it was Bill Russell's presence in the middle that psychologically affected the team and made them fear the Celtics.[xiv]

No other player in the history of the NBA at that time had the imposing and intimidating effect that Russell had on other teams and players. He was only one man, but every team feared the Celtics precisely because of him. Russell was simply the only man that had that kind of presence in the entire league—but not for long.

As Bill Russell and his Celtics were celebrating their second NBA championship, another gigantic center was making his way to the NBA after dominating the collegiate ranks for two seasons and before bringing his talents to the Harlem Globetrotters for one year. That man was the imposing and dominating force named Wilt Chamberlain.

He was not the same winner that Russell was in college but Chamberlain owned the collegiate ranks after Bill went on to proceed to the NBA. While Russell was known for his defense and rebounding, Chamberlain was a scoring and rebounding force that could also protect the basket. His ability to dominate games with his unstoppable inside scoring and his ability to own the rebounds were what made people call him the greatest individual player ever, even when he was just in college. There were those that claimed Wilt was better than Bill ever was even when he was still in college, and that was because no one was ever as dominant as Chamberlain was inside the paint.

Drafted by the Philadelphia Warriors with their territorial pick, Wilt Chamberlain was every bit the physical specimen that Bill Russell was. This gigantic 7'1" and 270-pound monster could jump through the roof and was a world-class sprinter himself. In other words, he was bigger and stronger but was just as great or perhaps even better of an athlete than Bill Russell.

But while they had similar athletic feats, Wilt was a lot bigger. He also had an impressive offensive repertoire that did not solely rely on his ability to tower and power over any other player on the floor. Instead, he had a smooth game down on the low post and could also hit turnaround jumpers with grace. But as big and offensively sound as Chamberlain was, Russell was the better player in terms of his defensive IQ because he understood how to cover the basket better than anyone else. Wilt was also a fantastic defensive player, but he mostly relied on his size and athletic gifts to protect the basket.

The first time Wilt Chamberlain stepped foot onto an NBA court in the 1959-60 season was the moment that made him the single-most imposing individual figure the league had ever seen. It was regular for him to put up 40 points and 40 rebounds on any given night. It also was not rare for him to be scoring 50 points, as no other center in the league was a match for Wilt— with the exception of Bill Russell, of course.

November 7, 1959, was the date when the two towering figures met for the first time on a basketball court. Their head-to-head matchup was billed as the "Battle of the Titans."[iv] Before that meeting, Chamberlain was averaging 40 points and 34 rebounds while shooting 47.5% from the floor. He was an unstoppable offensive force that used his size, strength, and athleticism to power shots over smaller defenders. But being the smart and physically capable defender that he was known as, Bill Russell took the challenge in stride.

Known for researching and studying his opponents' tendencies, Russell could frustrate Chamberlain into a comparatively poor offensive outing for the gigantic Warrior center. He used every bit of his 6'10" frame and 7'4" wingspan to make it difficult for Wilt to get an easy shot. It worked effectively, and the dominant rookie finished with 30 points on a dismal 12 out of 38 shooting from the field.

Bill, on the other hand, finished with the win and had 22 points and 35 rebounds. Round 1 of what was going to be the 1960s' most epic head-to-head rivalry went to Bill Russell. However, Wilt would exact his revenge on November 25th when he went for 45 points and 35 rebounds in a win for the Warriors. Those were only two of the many games that the two giants played that season.

While Russell continued his usual brand of dominant basketball on the defensive end, there was finally a player that could match or even exceed the physical feats that he displayed on the hardwood floor. Bill was every bit the dominant rebounder and rim protector he always was, but Wilt was on the same level in only his rookie season. The two giants were on a level all their own, and nobody else in the entire NBA could be mentioned in the same sentence as Bill Russell and Wilt Chamberlain. In that regard, the 60s era of the NBA was all about the two giants that were larger than life. Their battles were as legendary as the cinematic bouts between King Kong and Godzilla.

That said, Bill Russell finished the season averaging monstrous numbers of 18.2 points and 24 rebounds. But even though he had increased his rebounding rate that season, he did not lead the league in rebounds for the first time in his career. Wilt Chamberlain was averaging 27 boards a night as a rookie on top of the league record of 37.6 points he put in night in and night out. Russell also finished as runner-up to Chamberlain, who became the very first Rookie of the Year and MVP in the same season.

But even though Russell had become a statistical afterthought to what Chamberlain was doing from an individual perspective, the Boston Celtics were still on top of the NBA. Bill led his team to 59 wins, which was a new league record at that time. Even though he did not have the ridiculous numbers and individual accomplishments that Wilt had, Bill was continuing to make his team and everyone around him better.

That was the biggest difference between the two during the 60s. Bill Russell entered the NBA as part of an established roster that only needed him to complete their defense. He was a complementary piece that allowed everyone else on the team to focus on their tasks. On the other hand, Wilt Chamberlain *was* the team because he joined a roster that was in desperate need of a player who could dominate the floor on both ends of the court. And the difference between them was made clear in the postseason.

Bill and Wilt met in the playoffs as the Boston Celtics squared off with the Philadelphia Warriors in the Eastern Division Finals. That was the first of what would become many playoff meetings between the two legendary rivals and their teams. It was also one of the hardest-fought playoff battles between the two titans, as neither the Celtics nor the Warriors were willing to budge.

The series between the two went to six games. No matter how dominant Chamberlain was, he was merely one man versus a well-oiled and disciplined Boston Celtics team on the attack. Chamberlain, who averaged

30.5 points and 27.5 rebounds, may have won the individual matchup as far as stats were concerned, but individual stats do not always translate to wins. Russell's 20.7 points and 27 rebounds in that series were more than enough to kick the Warriors out of the playoffs. Bill might have been outscored by 81 points by the massive titan in Philadelphia, but he did enough to make things difficult for Wilt, who was limited to only 12 points in Game 3 of that series.

After that series win over the Philadelphia Warriors, the Boston Celtics met the St. Louis Hawks in the finals for the third time in four years. The series was as hard-fought as the previous two meetings between the two teams, as the grueling match went to seven games. But the Celtics were still the better team as they defeated the Hawks in a blowout in Game 7. Bill Russell had a fantastic series and even set a finals record of 40 rebounds in Game 2. And with that win, he also became a three-time NBA champion.

During the 1960-61 season, Bill Russell continued his consistent brand of basketball. He may have been dethroned as the NBA's best rebounder and greatest athletic and physical specimen, but that did not stop him from doing the things that made him the legendary basketball figure he always was. That included trying his best to stop Wilt Chamberlain in the many battles they had that season. In one of those games, Wilt even broke Bill's single-game record for most rebounds after he pulled down 55 boards against the Celtics on November 23, 1960. But Russell still did just enough to lead Boston to a win that night.

It was also during that season when Bill Russell scored his career high in points. Against no less than Wilt Chamberlain and the Philadelphia Warriors on March 5, 1961, Russell not only defended Chamberlain with all his might but also tried to match the bigger giant point for point in that epic duel. In that win over the Warriors, Bill came out with a career-best 37 points to go along with 25 rebounds, while Wilt finished with 47 points and 26 rebounds. That was the only time Bill Russell scored at least 30 points all season long.

At the end of the regular season, Russell averaged 16.9 points and 23.9 rebounds. Even though he failed to lead the league in rebounds again and Wilt Chamberlain was continuing to dominate the NBA with his scoring and rebounding numbers, Bill Russell was named the league's Most Valuable Player for the second time in his career. This was thanks to how he led his team to 57 wins that season.

That season's playoffs turned out to be the easiest Russell and his Celtics had since winning their first title in 1957. They made short work of the Syracuse Nationals in only five games in the Eastern Division Finals before meeting the St. Louis Hawks in the NBA Finals for the fourth time in five years. But the difference this time was that it was not a hard-fought battle. The Celtics had grown far too dominant and quickly dispatched the Hawks in five games to win a championship for the third consecutive season. That win gave Bill Russell his fourth NBA title in five years.

The 1961-62 season was truly the campaign that proved how valuable a leader and individual player Russell was to his team. He continued to do the things that Bill Russell was known to do but elevated his team to even greater heights as the Boston Celtics won a new NBA record of 60 regular season games. In the process, Russell averaged a career-best 18.9 points and 23.6 rebounds that season.

If one were to compare Bill Russell's numbers to what Wilt Chamberlain was doing that season, one would be surprised just how far the gap between the two players was in respect to individual numbers. That was the season when

Wilt put up his legendary unbreakable single-game record of 100 points. On top of that, he was averaging 50.4 points and 25.7 rebounds the entire season. No other player had even eclipsed 40 points per game in a single season, but Chamberlain was out there putting up 50 a night. That was more than double what Bill Russell was averaging all season long.

Furthermore, Wilt was not the only one averaging ridiculous numbers that season. Second-year guard Oscar Robertson was averaging 30.8 points, 12.5 rebounds, and 11.4 assists that season to become the first player in NBA history to average a triple-double in an entire season. It took until 2017 for another player to replicate that feat when Russell Westbrook averaged a triple-double in a single season for only the second time in more than 50 years. All that said, Bill Russell's individual numbers were not all that impressive compared to what Chamberlain and Robertson were doing.

However, even though there was this gigantic man averaging 50 points and 25 rebounds and an athletic marvel of a guard averaging a triple-double, the 1961-62 MVP trophy found its way back to the arms of Bill Russell for a second consecutive season. This only proved that individual stats do not define how valuable a player is to his team. Instead, you have to look outside the stats sheet and see how well the team performed around Russell to know how truly valuable of a player he was.

Russell might not have been the most refined offensive player, but he was a good enough scorer to put up great scoring numbers on any given night. However, he knew that scoring was not what the Boston Celtics needed from him. He was better off deferring the scoring load to better scorers such as Bob Cousy, Sam Jones, Tom Heinsohn, and Frank Ramsey instead of trying to match Wilt's numbers to prove that he was every bit the imposing giant as his rival was. Was he the league's best individual player? He was not. But did he add the most value to his team? He certainly did.

The simple logic of Russell's status as the MVP that season boiled down to the importance of his role on that team. Everyone knew that the Celtics played a team brand of basketball because all the players that were fielded by Red Auerbach had specific roles that they needed to play. Russell, of course, was the defensive anchor that defended the rim, blocked shots, and ignited the fast break. And he played his role to perfection, to the point that his value could never be understated.

Wilt and Oscar had their specific roles as well, and they were asked to play the role of the guys that did everything on their respective teams. Such players were incredibly valuable from a statistical standpoint, but their values were not up to par with how well their teams were performing. One could argue that the fact that Russell was contributing to the success of his team despite having a somewhat smaller role in comparison to Chamberlain and Robertson, and that was what truly cemented his place as the more valuable player to his team.

The late great Kobe Bryant, although a Laker legend, developed a great relationship with Bill Russell during the Celtics legend's latter years. Bryant once said that Russell understood what he needed to do as a defender because he had teammates that he knew were a lot better than him in the other aspects of the game. And while Russell believed that he could have been a good offensive player if he truly wanted to, he knew that it was better for him to allow his teammates to cover that part of the game because basketball was always a team sport.

"Russell said, 'What I do best is defend and rebound, so I'm going to completely focus on that. Let Cousy handle the ball. Let Jones be the shooter, Havlicek be the shooter,'" Bryant told *ESPN's* Jemele Hill in an interview. "And I thought that was a very, very insightful thing that I used in how I was able to go on and win those two championships."

As such, one of the many things that made Russell more valuable was his ability to own and play his role to perfection. A player did not have to do everything on the court to become truly valuable to his team. But because Russell knew that his value was on the defensive end of the floor, he made sure to perfect his ability to play defense to become truly indispensable to the Celtics. He was always completely selfless in his pursuit of a win for his team. And that was why everyone in the league respected him as a true MVP.

The three-time Most Valuable Player went on to meet his arch-rival in the playoffs for the second time in three seasons when the Boston Celtics clashed with the Philadelphia Warriors in the Eastern Division Finals. This meant that Bill Russell had the unenviable task of trying to slow down Wilt Chamberlain and his 50-point scoring average.

In one of the hardest-fought East Finals that Russell had to play, the Boston Celtics traded wins with the Philadelphia Warriors in their respective home arenas as the entire affair reached a pivotal seventh and deciding game. That was when Russell put on a defensive show of the ages. He denied Chamberlain possessions by bodying him up and making sure passes did not come his way. And when Wilt did get the ball, Bill made sure that he was far from his comfort zone or did not have a good look at the basket.

With Bill Russell playing a masterful defensive game against Wilt Chamberlain in Game 7, the Boston Celtics were able to escape with a two-point win. Russell limited Chamberlain to only 22 points on 7 out of 15 shooting that night while he himself contributed 19 points and 22 rebounds. Had he allowed even one or two more good looks for Wilt, things would have been different for the Boston Celtics. In fact, it was Sam Jones who saved the day for Boston when he made a clutch basket in the final few seconds of the game.

The Celtics were on their way to the NBA Finals for a sixth straight season and were set to meet the upstart Los Angeles Lakers for only the second time. Back then, they did not know that the 1962 NBA Finals paved the way for what was to become the hottest rivalry in all of basketball, as there would be several more championship battles between those two teams in the future.

Even after battling the St. Louis Hawks hard in the Western Division Finals, the Elgin Baylor and Jerry West-led Los Angeles Lakers were tough enough to force Game 7 in Boston against the mightiest team in the league. Game 7 was just as tough as the first six games on the part of Boston, as four of their main forwards were fouled out after they found it a difficult task to guard Elgin Baylor.

When the Lakers failed to win the series with a missed eight-foot shot, Russell put on a clutch performance in overtime as he was forcing Baylor to attempt tough shots. His defensive mastery over Baylor was what gave the Celtics enough cushion, as Russell led his team to a three-point win to clinch the series and the NBA championship once again. Bill Russell had a Game 7 to remember when he poured in 30 points and 40 rebounds to secure his fifth NBA championship title.

Coming into the 1962-63 season, Russell regained his title as the Eastern Division's most dominant center when the Warriors relocated to San

Francisco in the Western Division. Chamberlain playing out in the West meant that the two rivals did not have to meet as often in the regular season, and that the only way for them to battle it out in the playoffs again was for Wilt to lead his team to the NBA Finals. But even without his old nemesis to go up against, Bill Russell remained as competitive as ever.

The big man in the middle for the Boston Celtics led the team to 58 wins during the regular season. In doing so, Russell averaged 16.8 points and 23.6 rebounds for the league-leading Boston Celtics. For the fourth time in his career and a third consecutive season, Bill Russell was named the NBA's Most Valuable Player. And yes, he won the award even though Wilt was averaging ridiculously monstrous numbers of 44.8 points and 24.3 rebounds.

Boston escaped a hard-fought battle against Oscar Robertson and the Cincinnati Royals in the Eastern Division Finals as the series went to seven games. And in the NBA Finals, the Boston Celtics once again defeated the Los Angeles Lakers, and did so in six games as the rivalry between the two teams continued to grow. For five straight seasons and for the sixth time overall, Bill Russell and the Boston Celtics came out as the top team in the entire NBA.

Meeting Wilt in the Finals

Unfortunately for the Boston Celtics, they lost Bob Cousy to retirement entering the 1963-64 season. This meant that other guards such as K.C. Jones had to step up on the playmaking end. It also meant that Bill Russell had to take on a bigger leadership role because Cousy was responsible for a large part of that during his run with the Celtics. Cousy was the man that revolutionized the point guard position and paved the way for players like Magic Johnson, Steve Nash, and Chris Paul when it came to the position's pass-first mentality. And while Jones was a capable point guard himself, he was not at Cousy's level in terms of how well he orchestrated the offense for the Celtics.

But even without Bob Cousy, the Boston Celtics remained the most dominant team in the league that season. K.C. Jones, Sam Jones, and vastly-improved sixth man John Havlicek were picking up where Cousy left off as a playmaker and perimeter scorer. But more importantly, Bill Russell found himself playing the role of the facilitator more often. No longer was he confined to merely throwing outlet passes after a rebound. He had become a main playmaker from the post and consistently found open teammates with his vision and basketball IQ.

It was also that season when Bill Russell found himself back atop the rebounding ladder in the NBA, not only because he continued to improve as a rebounder but also because Wilt Chamberlain was sharing the Warriors' paint with fellow seven-footer and future Hall-of-Famer Nate Thurmond. For the first time since 1959, Russell would lead the NBA in rebounding and continued to be a dominant deterrent for the Celtics inside the paint.

After the 1963-64 regular season, Bill Russell averaged 15 points and a league-leading 24.7 rebounds. He also improved his assist numbers to 4.7 per game while leading the Boston Celtics to yet another top finish, not only in the Eastern Division but in the entire NBA. Was there ever a doubt that the Celtics were once again the title favorites?

In the Eastern Division Finals, the Boston Celtics made short work of the Cincinnati Royals by defeating them in only five games. Russell had a clutch performance in the fifth game after going for 20 points, 35 rebounds, and 7 assists to dispatch the Royals. And for the eighth consecutive season, he and his Celtics were on their way to the NBA Finals, where there awaited a familiar towering figure. This would be the first time Bill Russell met Wilt Chamberlain in the NBA championship series.

When you talk about the greatest debates in basketball history, it usually involves comparing one superstar to another. In the '80s, people often debated whether Magic Johnson or Larry Bird was better. In today's generation, there is the never-ending conversation about whether or not LeBron James has surpassed Michael Jordan as the greatest of all time. We also see modern-day conversations involving whether or not Nikola Jokic is better than Joel Embiid. However, most basketball minds would argue that the greatest debate in NBA history is who between Bill Russell and Wilt Chamberlain was the greater '60s center.

As you compare the two most prominent figures of the '60s, it is impossible not to see the contrast in styles and personality. They may have played the same position, but almost everything about Bill and Wilt was different. It might even be easier to point out their similarities than their differences. They were both athletic giants that rebounded the ball at phenomenal rates. They were also great at protecting the basket and blocking shots. But aside from that, they could never be any more different than they were.

History remembers Bill Russell as an intimidating defensive force in the paint that backed his teammates up with his terrific presence near the basket. He played the defensive end of the court as if he owned it. Russell was always patrolling the middle to prevent or deter players from trying to get too close to the basket by using his huge frame and long arms to block shots or alter attempts. And when everyone thought he was far away from the basket guarding his defensive assignment, he could instantly retreat back to the weak side to play help defense. In other words, there were no easy baskets as long as Russell was out on the floor.

Russell was not the most polished player on offense, but he was an opportunistic scorer that could put up points when he was open near the basket or when he has a good look after an offensive rebound. He was mostly utilized as an outlet passer that initiated the fast-break after completing defensive plays with a rebound. And at this point in his career, he had also improved exponentially as a facilitator from the post. In short, Russell knew that deferring to his teammates on offense was the better option for him.

Meanwhile, Wilt Chamberlain was the polar opposite out on the basketball court. While he was also an intimidating defensive presence that blocked shots and protected the basket, his energy was primarily reserved for the offensive end, especially during his younger years. Using his boundless energy, Chamberlain was always out there on the floor to make a difference on offense. And no one could question his cardiovascular abilities because he was playing 48 minutes a game year by year. And because he was bigger, faster, stronger, and much more athletic than any other player in the NBA, it was easy for him to muscle his way to the basket and dunk over his defenders.

The common consensus is that Wilt Chamberlain was just a brute that outmuscled everyone for easy points. However, a player cannot score 50 points a night on brute force alone. Wilt was also a highly skilled center that could hit turnaround jumpers and hook shots near the basket. Because the offense always went through him, he always had the ball in his hands and was also ready to make plays for his teammates. That said, Chamberlain was what a perfect scoring center should be like.

Off the court, the two players were also vastly different. Bill Russell never forgot his humble beginnings and stayed true to his foundations even when he was not playing basketball. He did not interact much with fans and always thought of himself as a competitor that had a lot of pride within. His life motto, "A man has to draw a line inside himself that he won't allow any man to cross," was passed down to him from his paternal grandfather and was the very essence of what he was as a person both on and off the court.[xv] That was why Russell never backed down from both authoritative figures and bigger players—because he never wanted anyone to step over his pride.

Russell also carried the same humility on the basketball court because he was a no-nonsense type of center that only did what needed to be done. Instead of doing any extra-curricular activities on and off the court, he focused on his role and what he needed to do to win championships. He made sure that he lived a life without distractions so that he could provide for himself and his family through the sport that had helped him escape a life of poverty.

On the other hand, Wilt Chamberlain was the star that loved being under the spotlight. He had grown used to the attention ever since he was in high school because basketball minds were already pegging him as the next big thing in the sport. Chamberlain loved going out at night to party and was frequently seen in New York when he was in Philadelphia. He simply loved the big stage, both on and off the court. Some would say that the gigantic Warriors center had a more colorful personality than Russell as well. They were opposites in almost every aspect of basketball and of life in general because Wilt wanted to be the man in the middle, both on and off the court. And who could blame him? Wilt was simply an elite superstar that had the personality of a true celebrity in every sense of the word.

That said, one can never mention the '60s era of the NBA without having to debate who between those two towering figures was the best player of that decade. Some say it was Wilt Chamberlain because of how he was putting up numbers that are still on the top of the NBA's record books to this date. However, a popular belief is that Bill Russell was the better giant because of his championships. Regardless of stats, Russell was the catalyst that enabled his team to win.

As far as championships were concerned, Russell was the most accomplished player, not only because he was a better leader but also because he had a better team that was already organized well enough when he got there. Meanwhile, Chamberlain entered a situation wherein he had to be "the man" because no one else on his team could help carry the load. And while Chamberlain was undoubtedly better when you looked at it from a purely one-on-one standpoint, no one made his team better than Russell did because the Celtics would not have been championship contenders every single season if he was not there to man the paint and anchor the defense.

Nonetheless, they had a 1964 Finals meeting to settle. Because Russell knew that his greatest strength was his defense and that the team needed him to focus on putting the clamps on Chamberlain, the three-time MVP made it his mission to limit his eternal rivals' production. Throughout the entire series, Russell used his body and quickness to deny Chamberlain the ball. And when he was unable to do so, he made it a point to push the big man out of his comfort zone so that he would not get good looks at the basket.

Defending Wilt was never an easy task, even for the greatest defensive player of all time. Russell was so used to using his length against opposing centers that may have been bulkier and stronger but were shorter. He was also more athletic than most of the other NBA centers of that decade. But he did not have any of those advantages against Wilt because The Stilt was younger, bigger, taller, stronger, and more athletic. That meant that Russell's defensive abilities were always tested whenever he had to bang bodies with Chamberlain down in the low post.

But while it may have been true that Chamberlain was a lot bigger and stronger than Russell, the Celtics center was more than just a tall and athletic body. Russell knew when to be physical when he needed to. He was not the strongest player but he could certainly hold his own against anyone down in the low block. And while it may be true that there is no true way to stop a prime Wilt Chamberlain from scoring, Bill Russell was the best at limiting and making life tough for him so that the gigantic big man would get tired early in the game.

Bill Russell's strategy worked. He only scored in double digits twice in the series but he was able to make life more difficult for Chamberlain. The Warriors' center was held down to 29.2 points per game in the entire series after averaging 37 points during the entire regular season. Bill also added 25.2 rebounds to his name to make it possible for his teammates to score on more possessions.

As the dust settled, the first battle between King Kong and Godzilla had come to a close. It was a quick win for the Boston Celtics as they defeated the San Francisco Warriors in only five games. It was Russell and the Celtics' seventh title in eight years. And because of the job that Russell and Nate Thurmond did, Russell claimed that the Boston Celtics had the best defense of all time.[i] Of course, the player manning that defense was none other than himself.

Bill Russell's ability to defend the paint was so advanced during that era that he was basically the only player in the NBA that could limit Wilt Chamberlain's production. As Tom Heinsohn once noted, Russell had a book on everyone in the league because he was keeping track of the different habits and skills of his opponents during an era when smartphones were still decades away from becoming mainstream. And Red Auerbach even said that no player in the NBA can fool Russell twice with the same move in the same season because he always found a way to counter a new move if he got tricked by it the first time.

In that regard, every single move that Chamberlain tried on Russell was defended well because the Celtics legend already knew how to stop all of the many moves that Wilt had in his arsenal after seeing him attempt those moves in their earlier encounters. The mental aspect of Russell's defensive abilities was what truly set him apart when it came to his ability to keep a giant like Wilt in check.

Some of the greatest defensive centers in league history disregarded the mental aspect of defense. Mutombo often used his length and athleticism to defend the basket because he was simply so much taller and longer than any other center in the league during his prime. Dwight Howard used his supreme athleticism and mobility to swat away shots with ease. And Rudy Gobert, a terrific defensive center himself, often played within the system and understood how to use his length to cover the basket.

But what separated Russell from all the other defensive centers was his ability to play the mental aspect of the game. As physically gifted a defender as he was, he also understood that there is also a mental aspect when it comes to playing defense. It was against Chamberlain in the finals and in the many different battles that they waged that Russell was able to use the mental aspect of defense to thwart The Stilt.

Russell understood that basketball was a team sport and that not even Chamberlain, for all his unworldly talents, was capable of defeating an entire team on his own. That was why there were instances wherein Russell simply allowed him to go and get his 40 points. In some instances, Wilt's goal was to put up 40 points on Russell's head, and it did not matter how many shots he took to get to that number. Russell understood this mental part of Chamberlain's game, and that was why he allowed him to score well in some instances but made sure to make things tough for him. If Wilt wanted 40 points, he had to take 40 shots—and some of those shots were tough attempts that he likely should have passed to his teammates that had better looks.

Kobe Bryant also once said that he learned from Bill Russell that the mind games between him and Wilt Chamberlain were deep. There were instances wherein Russell simply allowed Chamberlain to score because The Stilt, during his younger years, was at his happiest when he was putting up points. When Wilt did not have to work hard for his points, he was less motivated to win a game. But in the instances where Russell made him work for his numbers, Chamberlain's intensity was at an all-time high. Bill wanted a less-motivated, Wilt even if he had to allow him to score 30 points.[xvi]

"Psychologically, you have to try to make the offensive player question what he's doing," Russell said. "'Will this work? Can I make this shot?' You have to create doubts."

As such, Russell's ability to defend and make things tough for Chamberlain, the most unstoppable player in history, was more mental than physical. It was the mental aspect of the game that allowed him to win almost all his encounters with The Stilt. While Wilt was simply a lot more talented and skilled than him physically, Bill's ability to use the psychological aspect of the game allowed him to bridge the gap between them. The result? A championship win against Wilt in 1964.

Winning Eight Straight Titles

Even after winning six consecutive NBA championships, the Boston Celtics continued to stay hungry for more as Bill Russell and the entire team found new ways to improve both their offense and defense. Even though Bill Russell, K.C. Jones, Sam Jones, and Tom Heinsohn were aging into their 30s, it seemed as if they were still younger men that had a lot to prove.

On his part, Russell continued to look for his teammates instead of trying to score on his own. Sam Jones and John Havlicek became the focal point of the offensive attack as Bill was finding new ways to set his high-scoring teammates up for easier looks at the basket whether it was in transition from an outlet pass or on half court from the post.

Russell also continued to reign over the entire NBA on the rebounding end. He even had two 40-rebound performances that season. The first one was on March 11, 1965, against the Detroit Pistons. He finished that game with 27 points and 49 rebounds (his career-high was 51). The second one was against the Chamberlain-less San Francisco Warriors three days later. Russell had 20 points and 41 rebounds in that win for the Celtics.

With Bill Russell playing that way, he led the league in rebounding for a second consecutive season and for the fifth time overall. He averaged 14.1 points, 24.1 rebounds, and a new career high of 5.3 assists for the Boston Celtics, who accumulated a new NBA record of 62 wins that season. For his efforts in leading Boston to another fantastic regular season finish, Russell was named the NBA's Most Valuable Player for the fifth and final time in his career. In the entire history of the NBA, only Bill Russell, Kareem Abdul-Jabbar, and Michael Jordan have won five or more MVP awards.

The fact that Russell found himself as the only player in league history with five MVP awards at that time was proof of his incredible impact on his team. Despite the fact that he was not putting up the gaudy numbers that the younger NBA players of that era were posting, he was still the player that determined whether or not the Celtics had a chance to win. In comparison to the other players that were able to win five or more MVP awards, Russell's numbers were not all that impressive. But his impact was one that everyone in the league felt because opposing players knew that the Celtics would not have been as competitive if Russell was not playing at the highest level possible on the defensive end.

After a few years of not seeing any challenges in the Eastern Division Finals, Boston saw an up-and-coming contender. The Philadelphia 76ers, who had just relocated from Syracuse, acquired a disgruntled Wilt Chamberlain from San Francisco to bolster their lineup. Once again, it was Bill Russell versus Wilt Chamberlain in the playoffs.

The Philadelphia 76ers gave Russell and company some trouble in that series. That was because Wilt was no longer a one-man army on that 76ers team. He had a Hall-of-Fame teammate in Hal Greer and several other capable guys that could score and contribute on any given night. In a sense, Wilt had learned that he did not need to take matters into his own hands to win a game.

That series went to seven games as both teams traded wins on each of their respective home floors. It all came down to a seventh and deciding game in which one of the most legendary moments in NBA history happened. And what was strangest about that moment was that it did not involve Bill Russell, who was busy keeping his body on Wilt Chamberlain.

There were only five seconds left on the clock and the Celtics were up by a point against the Sixers. Boston had possession of the ball, but they turned it over and lost it out of bounds. Philadelphia had a chance to win the game with an inbound play in the final seconds of regulation. However, when legendary guard Hal Greer inbounded the ball, another future Hall-of-Famer saved the day for Boston by stealing the pass. That was when Celtics commentator Johnny Most uttered the all-time famous phrase, "Havlicek stole the ball! It's all over! Johnny Havlicek stole the ball!"[i]

This was the play that a lot of people would remember Havlicek for. There is no mistaking the fact that Havlicek ended up having one of the greatest careers a wing player could ever have. But it was that play that exemplified and ultimately solidified his legend. Of course, this was also a testament to how well-rounded that Celtics team was. Every player on that team played a role perfectly, and that included John Havlicek, who had a defining hero moment for Boston.

After that heroic defensive play from John Havlicek, the Boston Celtics would go on to the 1965 NBA Finals to meet the Los Angeles Lakers in a renewal of their rivalry. Russell and the Celtics had an easier time with the Lakers as they dispatched their foes in only five games to win the NBA Championship for the seventh consecutive season.

The 1965-66 season was one of the most difficult campaigns Bill Russell had in his entire career. Not only did he suffer minor injuries throughout the season, but age was beginning to catch up to him and the other core players such as Sam Jones and K.C. Jones. In fact, one of their top players, Tom

Heinsohn, had just retired following the 1965 championship win over the Lakers. This was when the Celtics were starting to show their mortality after winning championship after championship during the 60s. But the fighter in Russell was one of the things that allowed the Celtics to keep on competing against an NBA landscape that was becoming more and more competitive.

Nevertheless, Russell still looked and played better than most guys who were ten years younger than he was. He might have lost some of the quickness and athleticism that helped him become a dominant and imposing presence near the basket, but he already had ten years of NBA experience to know how to play defense in a smarter and more efficient way. At that point, his basketball IQ had become an even bigger weapon for him than his size and athleticism. So, even if he could no longer outrun all the other big men in the league or cover a defensive lapse in a split second, his incredibly high basketball IQ proved to be a weapon that allowed him to bridge the gap between himself and the younger players that were starting to take over the NBA.

Russell averaged a new career low of 12.9 points that season but still had great rebounding numbers of 22.8 in addition to the 4.8 assists he was dishing. The Celtics also declined that year and would only win 54 games throughout the regular season. For the first time in a long while, they were not the top team entering the playoffs. This meant that the road to the NBA Finals was not going to be as easy as it was in previous years.

That said, Bill Russell and the Boston Celtics battled the Cincinnati Royals in a hard-fought Eastern Division Semi-Finals to try to advance to the East Finals. They had a scare after falling 1-2 in the series but went on to win Games 4 and 5 to beat the Royals in five total games and keep their hopes of an eighth straight championship alive.

In the Division Finals, the Celtics met the Philadelphia 76ers again in yet another playoff battle that featured Bill Russell and Wilt Chamberlain. This time, however, the newly minted NBA MVP and his Sixers had home-court advantage, which had played a crucial role in the seven-game series they played against the Celtics in the previous season. Chamberlain had also changed his game quite a bit that season because he was starting to trust his teammates more than he ever did in his career. Wilt was still the league's best scorer but he was no longer the man that sought to score 40 or more per game as he realized that there was more to being an NBA player than being a great scorer.

But even though the Sixers had home-court advantage, Russell and the Celtics had seemingly figured their opponents out. Bill limited Wilt, who was averaging more than 33 points per game during the regular season, to only 23.5 points in the first four games of that series. Although he allowed Chamberlain to score 46 points in Game 5, it was a wasted effort as the Boston Celtics defeated the Philadelphia 76ers in only five games to advance to the NBA Finals for the eighth straight time.

The 1966 NBA Finals against the Los Angeles Lakers was a weird one for Bill Russell. That series saw him scoring more points than he ever had in the finals, and no one on the Lakers' roster was a physical match for him down in the middle. But, even with Bill putting on a good scoring performance, the series went to seven games. Game 7 went down to the wire as the Boston Celtics narrowly escaped with a two-point win to secure their eighth straight championship and ninth title in total.

At the age of 31, Bill Russell averaged 23.6 points and 24.3 rebounds in arguably his greatest performance in all of the finals series that he played in. This was a testament to how much he had evolved as an NBA player because he could change his game and adjust to the flow depending on the looks that the opposing team was giving him. And because he understood that the Lakers were looking to slow the guards and wings instead of defending him, he took advantage of Leroy Ellis and Darrall Imhoff to help his teammates in that series, as he led the Celtics in scoring and rebounding in those seven games.

But while the Celtics still lorded over the entire NBA after winning eight straight championships in 1966, they eventually learned that the entire league was already keeping up with them. Boston's age was showing despite the fact that the future was basically secured, with John Havlicek rising up as the star that the Celtics would rely on in future seasons. But the increasingly competitive NBA landscape was catching up. And, of course, Russell was already 31, which may not be that old by today's modern standards because of the advancements in medicine and athletic training, but it was already quite ancient back then.

But the worst part was not that the Celtics were aging. Instead, they had to look at the team's coaching staff to understand that the days of the dynasty were finally closing. Yes, Red Auerbach had already decided that he had won enough championships to call it a career. And while Bill Russell was the on-court anchor and leader that everyone relied on, Auerbach was the man responsible for building that team and turning it into a dynasty.

The Playing Coach, Losing to Wilt, The End of the Streak

After winning his eighth straight championship and ninth-overall title as the head coach of the Boston Celtics, Red Auerbach announced his retirement before the start of the 1966-67 season to play a bigger role in the franchise's front office. He wanted one of his former players to succeed him as the head coach, but they all rejected the offer.

Bob Cousy did not like the idea of coaching his former teammates. Meanwhile, Tom Heinsohn thought he could not handle Bill Russell. After all, Russell was still apprehensive of white authority figures despite playing for Auerbach his entire NBA career. He still needed a coach to earn his trust. Heinsohn probably did not think that he could earn Russell's trust. Nevertheless, he told Red to offer the job to Bill, despite the fact that the Boston center was still playing.[iv]

To that end, Red Auerbach gave the proposition to Bill Russell, who agreed to become the Boston Celtics' playing head coach. With that, Bill Russell became the first African-American head coach in the history of the NBA. He told reporters that he was given the job not because Red Auerbach wanted to make history but because the legendary head coach thought he had the leadership skills and basketball IQ to succeed at the helm of the Celtics.[iv]

The fact that Russell became the first Black American to coach in the NBA was surprising and groundbreaking already. But what was even more amazing was the fact that he was still playing while coaching the team. This has happened in the past, but most of the players that took on the role of head coach of their teams were not playing on championship-contending teams. Meanwhile, Russell was now in the shoes of a man who needed to coach his team to nine straight championships. As such, it was an entirely new challenge for him at that point in his career.

Though Russell had to work double-time as both the Celtics' head coach and best player, Boston actually improved from their previous season. This was not only because Russell handled the team so well in his first year as the head coach but also because of other factors such as John Havlicek's continued improvement and the acquisition of All-Star forward Bailey Howell. The Boston Celtics went on to win 60 games during the regular season. As a playing head coach, Russell averaged 13.3 points, 21 rebounds, and a career-high 5.8 assists.

Because Russell and the Celtics finished second in the Eastern Division during the regular season, they had to battle with the New York Knickerbockers to determine who was going to the Division Finals. The Boston Celtics quickly eliminated their foes in four games to secure a date with Wilt Chamberlain and the Philadelphia 76ers in the Eastern Division Finals for a third straight season.

That season, the Philadelphia 76ers had won a new league record of 68 wins. But this was not because Chamberlain was carrying the team on his back all season long. Instead, this was because Wilt himself transitioned from being a monstrous beast that scored all the points himself to becoming a more well-rounded player who had learned how to defer to his teammates and set them up. That was the first time in eight seasons that Wilt did not lead the league in points. However, the Sixers were actually better with Chamberlain playing the roles of defender, rebounder, and facilitator.

At that point in his career, Chamberlain took a few pages from Bill Russell's book by working more on his ability as a leader that could take his teammates to new heights. Instead of trying to score the ball on every possession, he made it a point to look for his teammates. But of course, opposing defenses were still wary of Wilt's ability to score the ball, and that was why he was the perfect decoy for the Sixers. And because he challenged himself that he could do more than just scoring, he made history by being the only center in league history at that time to average seven or more assists. It took until 2019 for Nikola Jokic to replicate that season.

Now, this was an entirely different challenge that Bill Russell needed to overcome. In the previous times he had faced Wilt Chamberlain, he understood the psyche of the giant because he knew that The Stilt was looking to score the ball every single time he had it in his hands. As a result, Russell's goal was to make Chamberlain work for his points while allowing him to subconsciously alienate his teammates from the play.

But the fact that Chamberlain had transformed into a player that understood the importance of knowing when to pass the ball and when to go for a basket was what turned him into a new puzzle that Russell needed to solve. It was easy for Russell to solve a person's offensive habits because no move could work on him the second time. He did his homework to make sure that he could find a way to stop a player's moves and make his opponents try to find new ways to score on him. But it was more difficult to learn how to defend a player that went for a pass instead of a shot because defending a pass had to be the effort of the entire time. So, even if Russell could defend Chamberlain's scoring abilities one-on-one, his teammates needed to find a way to defend his playmaking abilities.

A 50-point-scoring Wilt Chamberlain was not enough to beat the Boston Celtics in the past, but a more balanced version of the giant was what eventually turned out to be the bane of Bill Russell and his team. The Sixers took a page out of the Celtics' playbook and transformed into a more well-rounded team with scorers surrounding Wilt. Meanwhile, the legendary giant in the middle was a decoy that looked to set his teammates up first rather than to try to score against Bill Russell's defense. It worked because Russell was no longer just defending Wilt's scoring. Instead, he had to work hard to make sure that he was taking away Chamberlain's passing lanes as well. And the hard pill to swallow was the fact that Wilt had seemingly found a way to finally defeat Bill.

For the first time in his career, Bill Russell lost to Wilt Chamberlain in the playoffs. The Sixers' MVP averaged a triple-double of 21.6 points, 32 rebounds, and 10 assists to beat Russell and the Celtics in only five games. Chamberlain had finally removed a thorn in his side and became the better individual and team player that season. So, even if Wilt was not scoring a lot in that series, he did everything else at a high level. And that was when he finally found out that being a team-first player could beat the greatest defensive player in the history of the game.

On Bill Russell's part, that was the very first real loss he suffered in the playoffs, as most people do not count the 1958 Finals loss due to the foot injury that had hindered him. But Russell was not a sore loser. Instead, he visited Wilt Chamberlain in the 76ers' locker room and personally congratulated and shook the bigger man's hand and said one word: "Great." [iv]

It was a simple yet grand gesture coming from a legendary center to a man he had always considered his rival. And despite all the time they spent battling each other out on the court, the two would eventually become friends later in the future.

Losing to the best individual player of his era was not a knock on Russell's resume because he had already proven himself a real winner at that point in his career. He already proved himself the greatest team player at that point in NBA history because he won eight straight championships, a feat still unprecedented in today's era. No one can win every single time, and Russell learned that when he lost to Chamberlain for the very first time in the playoffs. But, ever the good sport, he was happy enough to see his eternal rival getting a chance to win the championship that he was yet to win at that point in his career.

However, the night was not yet over for Bill Russell. Clearly still in shock from that loss, he had his grandfather accompany him to the Boston Celtics' locker room. When they got in, they saw John Havlicek and Sam Jones showering next to each other while candidly talking and discussing the game. Jake, Bill's grandfather, broke down in tears instantly and told the younger Russell how happy he was that his grandson was the coach of a team where people of different colors treated each other as equals.[iv] Bill Russell might not have won the championship that season, but seeing how proud his grandfather was of him was a victory in its own right.

This was a special victory for Russell because he grew up in a family that experienced its fair share of racism in the past. Russell's grandfather, of course, lived during a time when racism was far worse than what Bill experienced during his days. It meant a lot for Bill to see that his grandfather was happy about the fact that he was working for an organization that broke boundaries and did not care about a person's race. And what was even better was that all of the players on that team cared for one another like true brothers under the leadership of a black man.

Return to the Top of the NBA, Bill Russell's Final Seasons

The road back to the peak of the league had grown even more difficult for Bill Russell and the Boston Celtics. Both Russell and Sam Jones were already 34 during the 1967-68 regular season and were not looking like their spry selves from ten years ago. K.C. Jones had just retired following the loss to the Sixers in the 1967 Eastern Finals to leave Bill and Sam as the only two players remaining from the core that had started the dynasty.

Age and wear evidently had a significant effect on Bill Russell that season, as the big man seemed weary and slow at times. His numbers continued to drop as his ability to play heavy minutes also declined. Russell averaged career lows of 12.5 points and 18.6 rebounds that season. (Of course, those might be career lows for a 34-year-old veteran, but Russell's numbers were still better than what most of the younger and bigger centers could put up in the NBA at that time.)

More and more talented big men were now entering the league. Wilt was still very much a threat to the Celtics. Meanwhile, Jerry Lucas was making a name for himself as one of the rising big men in the league. And Nate Thurmond was also becoming one of the best rebounders in the league as he was one of the few people that could average 20 rebounds a game.

In that regard, Russell was at an age where he should have been ready to cede the mantle over to the next generation. He was no longer the same dominant entity that he was in his younger years. But age allowed him to develop the experience and IQ necessary for him to anchor the defense of the Boston Celtics despite how the team had become much slower compared to its earlier years. And despite his advanced age, his competitive spirit never diminished.

Old as he was, Bill Russell coached and led his team to a 54-win season. Gone were the days when he could lead the Celtics to 60 wins a season. But that was understandable because Boston had lost some of the core members of its dynasty. The team was slowly shifting toward the future, especially with Havlicek still in the prime of his life. But Russell and Jones were already elder statesmen in the league and were basically dinosaurs that were one footstep outside of the retirement door. That was what made the quest for more championships challenging for the Celtics.

As expected, the playoffs were not going to be easy for the Boston Celtics. The Detroit Pistons managed to push their Division Semi-Finals series to six games. At one point, the Celtics were even down in the series before they won Games 4 to 6 to eliminate the Pistons and to proceed to the Division Finals for another date with Wilt Chamberlain and the Philadelphia 76ers.

That series against the Sixers was one of the finest moments on the part of the Boston Celtics. It also showed Bill Russell's grit and determination to get over his rival and return to the top of the NBA. This was because the Boston Celtics fell down 1-3 in the series and many already believed them to be down and out of the playoffs. Nobody in the history of the NBA at that time had ever come back from a 1-3 deficit in a seven-game series.

At one point in the series, basketball critics were saying that Bill Russell was already out of gas and that he had one foot out of the door toward retirement. This was because, despite all the battles he had waged with Wilt Chamberlain since 1959, he did not assign himself to defend the giant. Instead, the unenviable task of guarding Wilt went to backup center Wayne Embry. To this end, the press even said that Chamberlain had already worn Russell out from Games 1 to 4, as the Sixers were just one win away from making a return trip to the NBA Finals.

Embry, a veteran in the NBA at that time, had experienced a lot of hardships while playing for the Cincinnati Royals during his first eight seasons in the NBA. He used to be a double-double machine and was a spectacular presence down on the low post when he was playing alongside Oscar

Robertson. And while he was only 6'8", he had the strength and girth that allowed him to hold his own against a gigantic man like Chamberlain.

So, in a pure basketball sense, Russell had made the right choice to allow Embry to defend Chamberlain because he had the strength that allowed him to bang bodies with the legendary giant. Meanwhile, Russell played his usual role of protecting the basket as the greatest help defender that the league had ever seen. And it was his ability to play this role at the highest level that gave the Celtics a fighting chance, despite the fact that he was seemingly gassed and tired.

Luck and grit were on the side of the Celtics. Seemingly looking like a passing-of-the-torch moment, John Havlicek took over Games 5 and 6 after a dismal performance in Game 4. On top of that, the Philadelphia 76ers struggled to shoot from the floor in those two chances to close the series out as the Boston Celtics were able to force Game 7.

In Game 7, Bill Russell proved that he was not the tired old man people were calling him at that point in his career. He gave himself the task of defending Wilt Chamberlain and owned that defensive assignment from the first tip all the way to the final seconds. He was so good at denying Wilt good looks and possessions that the 76ers center was limited to only two shot attempts in the entire second half. But even denying Chamberlain was not enough to seal the deal for the Celtics as they were only up by two points in the final few seconds of the game.

Bill Russell was once again the force that made all the difference for the Boston Celtics in those last 34 seconds. He blocked a shot that might have tied the game up. And the moment he grabbed the rebound after another missed Sixers shot, he threw a pass to the 34-year-old Sam Jones for a layup that eventually gave the Boston Celtics a four-point win.

No one ever thought that Russell still had enough gas left in the tank to perform at the highest level when the lights were bright. But he had evidently saved his best performance for last when he made the difference in that series win against the Philadelphia 76ers. As such, Boston also became the very first team in the NBA to come back from a 1-3 series deficit to win it all. When a team has Bill Russell anchoring the paint, anything is possible.

In the NBA Finals, the Boston Celtics once again defeated the Los Angeles Lakers as Bill Russell was crowned a ten-time NBA champion in the 12 years he had played in the league. After just one year, it did not take long for the Celtics to return to the top of the NBA even after losing key players to retirement. And giving credit where credit was due, the Los Angeles Lakers star guard Jerry West (who later became the model for the NBA's logo) said that Bill Russell was his top choice as a teammate if ever he was given that chance. This was a testament to Russell's hard work, leadership, and determination to win basketball games.[xii]

Opponents respected Bill Russell as much as he respected them. Of course, the respect started from Russell, who did his homework on a daily basis to make sure that he got his defensive assignment right and that he knew how to stop the opposing team's best players. The work he poured into his craft was the ultimate sign of respect from Russell because he understood that he needed to respect his opponents if he wanted to learn how to defend them. And because opposing players knew how hard Russell worked on and off the floor to stop the opposing team from scoring, they respected him as well.

That was the case for Jerry West, who was one of the most spectacular offensive forces in the NBA at that time, despite being a lot smaller than the other players in the league. West had seen his fair share of Russell and the Celtics in the finals to understand that the Boston center was a consummate winner that knew what it meant to compete at the highest level. And because West was an accomplished competitor as well, he respected Russell's ability to defy the odds to win championships.

But soon enough, age and weariness had caught up to Bill Russell. The 1968-69 season was a problematic one for the playing head coach. He found himself getting tired a lot faster than before and was always feeling like he had already run out of gas. On top of that, all the banging and pounding with the giants of the NBA had affected his body and he was feeling all sorts of aches and pains.

True enough, the hard grind of constantly playing over 40 minutes a game while playing with a seemingly unlimited amount of energy on the defensive end had affected Bill Russell's body. Doctors said that his body was already fatigued.[iv] Nevertheless, the body follows where the mind goes, as Bill Russell managed to will his 35-year-old self to finish the season in one piece. For an elder statesman in the NBA, his 9.9 points and 19.3 rebounds were still very impressive.

However, the Boston Celtics finished the regular season with only 48 wins as against 34 losses. That was the worst record they have ever had in the Bill Russell era. That was because their core had already aged deep into their 30s. That said, the odds were stacked against the defending champions as they entered the playoffs with only the fourth seed in the East.

The fact was, the window was already closing on the Boston Celtics' dynasty. All of the greatest dynasties in the history of our world eventually ended, and that was the same case for the Celtics. There was only so much that this team could do to try to win another championship because Russell and Jones were aging. Meanwhile, they were yet to find a player that could hopefully serve as the replacement for Bill Russell as the anchor of their defense. While Havlicek had become the team's best player, the game of basketball was still a big man's league at that time. So, if the Celtics wanted to continue to compete in the future, they needed a center that could do at least half of what Russell was capable of.

But not even age was going to stop Russell from competing during the 1969 Playoffs. He was always defiant when it came to his limits because he was not going to allow anyone to tell him what he could or could not do. And teams in the league had to learn the hard way that Bill Russell was still willing to do whatever it took to win another championship.

For yet another year, the Boston Celtics met the Philadelphia 76ers in the playoffs. This time, however, there was no Wilt Chamberlain—yet. The giant had moved on from Philly and was now in Los Angeles. This made the series easy for the Celtics, who defeated the Sixers in only four games as they proceeded to the Division Finals against a vastly improved New York Knicks, whom they then defeated in six games to secure a date with the Los Angeles Lakers for another battle of the eternal rivals.

Adding color to the growing rivalry between the Celtics and the Lakers was Wilt Chamberlain, who had become the newest Lakers star. With Wilt in the picture, the Los Angeles Lakers were essentially a team of three all-time great superstars that had teamed up after years of struggling against Bill

Russell and the Boston Celtics. Because of that, the Lakers were the heavy favorites to dethrone the Celtics.

In the first two games, it seemed as if the Lakers were on their way to a quick Finals win after securing Games 1 and 2. That was largely thanks to Jerry West's combined 94-point outing in both those games as Bill Russell decided not to double-team the NBA's best guard and premier perimeter scoring threat. But things changed in Game 3 after Russell decided to put an extra defender on the spitfire shooter. Then, in Game 4, the 35-year-old Sam Jones sank a buzzer-beater off a triple-screen play drawn up by Russell to tie the series 2-2.

The series went to Game 7 and the Los Angeles Lakers were confident enough to win that one in LA and even scheduled a victory ceremony for the team on the game leaflets. Bill Russell used this bravado as a way to motivate his team. He told his players and teammates to go back to their roots and play a running style of basketball because, according to him, the more determined team was going to win Game 7. True enough, the Celtics were determined enough to hold on to their lead even as the Lakers rallied to Jerry West's outstanding performance.

John Havlicek's boundless stamina allowed him to set the pace for the team's running style in Game 7. Meanwhile, Russell defended the basket and secured the rebounds to fuel the team's transition attack. The 35-year-old Sam Jones also did his part by running as hard as he could whenever there was a chance for them to score in transition. And this tactic caught the Lakers by surprise because they did not think that an older Celtics team was willing to try to outrun them.

The strategy worked for the Celtics in what was a tightly contested Game 7. As the dust settled, the Los Angeles Lakers fell on their home floor to the Boston Celtics. Bill Russell had just secured his 11th and final NBA championship ring. And as a sign of sportsmanship, he went over to an exhausted and visibly downhearted Jerry West (who had won Finals MVP even while playing for the losing team) to try to console him.[iv] That was the last time West and the Lakers saw Bill Russell on an NBA hardwood floor. In fact, everyone in the world saw Russell as an NBA player for the final time in that seventh game in Los Angeles.

When the Boston Celtics returned to their hometown, they were greeted with cheers by some of the best fans in all of basketball. However, the coach and player that was largely responsible for bringing 11 NBA championships to the Boston Celtics was nowhere to be found. Russell did not attend the welcome party that awaited the Celtics in Boston. That was because he had already decided to retire from basketball and leave everything behind him. Russell left and never said a single word, believing that he did not owe the public anything.[iv] However, it was only because Bill was a man that did not like a lot of fuss. He wanted to go out quietly and without all the fanfare.[xvii]

Like a cloud of dust in the wind, Bill Russell was gone from the Boston Celtics in an instant. Not even his good friend and former head coach Red Auerbach was aware of what was going through the mind of the legendary center when he left the organization without a single word. This brought the once-great Boston Celtics franchise down to earth. After all, they did not have a coach entering the 1969-70 season and had already made free agency and draft choices thinking that Russell was still returning for at least one more season.[iv] Auerbach said that he would have drafted a center instead of drafting Jo Jo White had he known that Russell was going to retire at the end of the 1968-69 season.

This was one of the weirdest ways for someone of Russell's caliber to leave the game of basketball. Even back then, most stars announced their retirement ahead of time. Of course, Russell believed that he did not owe anyone anything. That was understandable back then because of the things that he went through during his younger years. But had he been vocal about his plans, the Celtics would have been able to prepare for the future ahead of time.

While Russell's final moments with the Boston Celtics were triumphant, history often forgets the abrupt way that he parted ways with his team. That is because history only remembers him as the perennial winner with 11 championship rings. History documents him as the man that anchored the NBA's greatest dynasty. And it remembers him as a man who is synonymous with greatness.

It took a while for the Celtics to recover from Bill Russell's departure because no one was good enough to fill the hole that he left in the team's center position. During a day and age when the center position was still the most important role in the game of basketball, the Celtics struggled to win games because they no longer had the greatest defensive player in history protecting the basket and securing rebounds. As such, it was only during the 1970-71 season when the team drafted Dave Cowens that the Celtics were able to return to championship contention. But even though Cowens was a great rebounder and a better scorer, he just did not have the defensive presence that made Bill Russell the greatest winner in the history of basketball.

After Retirement

After Bill Russell left the Celtics in 1969, his No. 6 jersey was retired on March 12, 1972. It was a private ceremony that did not have a lot of attendees. After all, Russell was known for keeping his silence during press conferences and did not mesh well with some media personalities. He did not like media and fan attention. In fact, only the Celtics that had a chance to play with Bill and the people in the organization closest to him were there to witness the banner raising.[xiv]

Bill Russell also had short coaching stints after retiring. He coached the Seattle SuperSonics from 1973 to 1977 and compiled a losing record of 162 wins as against 166 losses. It was not a successful coaching stint because he tried to implement the same style he used with the Celtics even though the system did not fit the Sonics' personnel. However, he did, in fact, lead that team to a playoff appearance.

In the middle of coaching the Sonics in 1975, Russell was inducted into the Naismith Basketball Hall of Fame. In effect, Russell was immortalized as one of the greatest figures in the history of this great sport. However, similar to his jersey retirement ceremony, he opted not to attend his Hall of Fame enshrinement due to his negative relationship with the media and his indifference to the attention and fanfare.

After coaching the Seattle SuperSonics, Bill Russell did try his hand at commentating on television but felt like it was not the best place for him to be at. He thought that his knowledge about the game of basketball could not be expressed in the time he had as a commentator.[iv] To that end, Russell went on to co-author several books about basketball and his life.

Bill Russell's last coaching stint was with the Sacramento Kings from 1987 to 1988. His time there was short-lived as he ended his coaching career with the Kings with a 17-41 record. After that, Bill Russell would never coach a professional basketball team again.

During the '90s, Russell lived a reclusive, silent, and peaceful life outside of the radar of the media. You hardly heard anything about him and what he was doing during that decade. But during the 2000s, he finally came out of his shell and could finally face the media and general public again. He even received several honors during that time and was named a founding member of the National Collegiate Basketball Hall of Fame and the FIBA Hall of Fame.

Then, on February 14, 2009, Bill Russell received the highest honor any individual player can ever get. The NBA Finals MVP was renamed the Bill Russell Finals Most Valuable Player Award. Kobe Bryant was the inaugural winner of that award. No other NBA player has ever been given the honor of getting an award named after him. And even though Russell never had the chance to be named Finals MVP (since the award was first given out in his final year in 1969), having that award named after him was what validated his status as the single greatest winner in NBA history.

Bill Russell was also named to all the anniversary teams of the NBA. He was a part of the 25th Anniversary Team in 1971, the 35th Anniversary Team in 1980, the 50th Anniversary Team in 1996, and the 75th Anniversary Team in 2021. That means that Russell's legendary status was respected by all the people that chose the select few who deserved to be immortalized as the greatest players of all time.

Chapter 5: Personal Life

Bill Russell's parents were Charles Russell and Katie Russell. Growing up, it was not uncommon for Bill to witness his parents getting treated differently because of the rampant racial discrimination in Monroe, Louisiana. His parents' experiences, as well as his, were what made Bill Russell a prominent figure in the African-American civil rights movement.

Russell met his first wife when he was still in college. His college girlfriend, Rose Swisher, became his wife in 1956 and they were together until 1973 when they divorced. Despite the long marriage, the couple already had problems as early as when Bill was still playing for the Celtics. Nevertheless, Bill was a devoted family man and the couple raised three exceptional children, a daughter named Karen and two sons, William Jr. and Jacob. Karen is perhaps the most well-known of their children, as she graduated from Harvard with a law degree and went on to devote her life to racial equality, much like her father.

In 1977, Bill got remarried to 1968 Miss USA, Dorothy Anstett. The marriage was short-lived and they eventually divorced in 1980. It took until 1996 for Bill Russell to remarry once again. Russell's third wife was Marilyn Nault, who stayed with Bill until her death in 2009.

Outside of basketball, Bill Russell was vocal and active in movements aimed toward bringing an end to racial discrimination, and this was primarily because of the experiences he and his family had in the past. Racism was also one of the reasons why Bill Russell was never all that fond of the Boston area. Sadly, he had bad experiences there even when he was the star of the Celtics. He wrote several accounts of his encounters with racism in his books. In 2011, he was awarded the Presidential Medal of Freedom by Barack Obama.

After becoming more active in the NBA as one of the people often featured whenever there were big games (especially the NBA Finals), Bill Russell lived a more secluded life, especially during the middle of the COVID-19 pandemic, which started in 2020. This was mainly due to his very advanced age. It was during the middle of the pandemic that Bill Russell died at the age of 88. He passed away at his Mercer Island home on July 31, 2022. His family never disclosed the cause of death. In a statement, NBA Commissioner Adam Silver called Russell "the greatest champion in all of team sports."

Chapter 6: Impact on Basketball

To say that Bill Russell is one of the trailblazers of the modern-day style of basketball is an understatement of what this legendary center has done for the sport and the NBA. Russell changed a lot of things in basketball with his dominating style of defense and insatiable strive for greatness as a winner.

Bill Russell's biggest impact on basketball was how much of a difference he made in the way defense was being played. Before Russell's rise to prominence, most players would play defense with their feet on the ground and would not even try to jump up for blocks because it allowed them to more quickly react to passes. But Bill Russell changed all of that.

The Celtics legend was one of the few players that blocked or altered shots by jumping up. Using his long arms and freakish athleticism, it was easy for Russell to swat away attempts at the basket. His high basketball IQ, preparation and knowledge of opponent tendencies, and terrific timing all helped make him a great rim protector as well.

After that, everyone seemed to have followed suit and tried to block or contest a shot at the apex—but no other player did it better than Bill himself. In a sense, Russell was the '60s version of great shot-blockers and rim protectors such as Hakeem Olajuwon, David Robinson, Dikembe Mutombo, Dwight Howard, and Rudy Gobert. But he was even better than them because of the way that he blocked the shots of his opponents and because he had athletic capabilities that were way ahead of his time.

Unlike some of the slow-footed seven-footers that have become great shot-blockers, Russell was uniquely ahead of his era. He might have blocked shots like Olajuwon and Mutombo, but his ability to play defense was far more than just his terrific skills at protecting the basket. He was more of an all-around defensive presence rather than just a mere paint defender.

With his quick foot speed and freakish acceleration, Russell was an athletic marvel that no other player could match during his time. He used his speed and quickness to move around the court so well that he could cover a seemingly impossible amount of ground in an instant. At one moment, you might think he is on a far spot on the court bodying up his defensive assignment. However, he could instantly run up to an open man to try to contest a shot at the basket. He was so quick on the defensive end that all his teammates had to do was to yell "Hey, Bill" for him to help out on defense and still recover quickly to his assignment in case of a pass.

But the best part about Russell's ability to defend was his presence of mind. In today's NBA, a lot of shot-blocking big men swat away shots like they are playing volleyball. Their style of blocking shots often makes the daily highlights because they swat the ball with such strength and ferocity that it often finds its way out of bounds. However, Russell made a conscious effort to make sure that his blocks triggered fast-break opportunities. He blocked shots in a manner that allowed the ball to stay in play. As such, he basically passed the ball to his teammates whenever he blocked opposing shots so that his teammates could get a running start. This style of defense was one that was exclusive to Russell due to his combination of size, length, athleticism, and IQ.

Due to his amazing physical gifts, Russell's build, wingspan, agility, quickness, and athleticism were similar to Anthony Davis, who can guard all positions out on the court because of his freakish physical gifts. That said, Russell was certainly ahead of his time because his all-around defensive abilities were not only confined to denying seven-footers like Wilt

Chamberlain open looks. Instead, he could defend multiple positions and even cover all players out on the court in one defensive possession, similar to how Draymond Green does in the modern NBA.

John Havlicek once said that Bill Russell's versatility and IQ as a defender helped him well enough to stop a three-on-one fast-break opportunity all by himself. He studied opponent tendencies carefully and could make players uncomfortable to score on him even when he was all alone in defending the transition attempt. In Havlicek's words, Russell could decrease a 90% scoring chance down to 50% because of how well he read offensive plays and player tendencies.[xii]

But despite all his abilities as a versatile defender, Bill Russell was still widely known as a one-on-one stopper that gave opposing big men nightmares. The one player that comes to mind is typically Wilt Chamberlain, who had easy outings when matched up with other centers but usually played subpar when battling against Bill Russell.

Former Celtics player Frank Ramsey describes it best. When Wilt was against other centers, he was never hesitant to instantly go up for a shot because he knew that he would not get blocked by any other player. However, he usually changed his tendencies when matched up with Bill. Chamberlain often tried to fake a shot first to try to get Russell off his feet because he knew that if he went up right away with his shot, there was a significant chance that Bill would block it in a heartbeat.

The mental aspect of defending Wilt was also one of the things that allowed Bill Russell to excel as the only man that could slow down the most dominant inside force the league has ever seen. He made it a point to switch things up when defending Chamberlain to keep the gigantic man guessing.

There were times when he tried to make Wilt work for his shots such that the giant had to go for 40 shots to score 40. This worked because it allowed Russell to force Chamberlain to alienate all of his teammates just so he could get his points. But there were instances when he simply allowed Wilt to get his points easily because he understood that the competitor in Chamberlain was more motivated when he had to work harder for those points.

It was the fact that Russell was such a cerebral defender that made him one of the most special players the league has ever seen. There are not a lot of cerebral players that look at the game of basketball from both a physical and a mental aspect, and Russell was one of them. Another example was Kobe Bryant, who worked just as hard as Russell did to find out what made their opponents tick and what they could do to make life tougher for them. It was the very fact that Bryant knew that Russell was the pioneer of the cerebral part of the game that made him idolize the Celtics legend. They ended up becoming great friends because Kobe tried to get some ideas on how Bill approached the game from a mental standpoint during his time.

That said, Bill Russell made an impact on the game of basketball by changing the very definition of what it is to become a great all-around defender. In fact, the way Russell defended back in the 60s is still the way most centers and big men defend the basket in today's NBA game. This means that, even though Russell played in a comparatively weaker era, he would still thrive in the modern-day league.

Red Auerbach said that he did not think that Bill Russell would be any less of a great player and competitor had he been placed in the '80s or '90s.[xii] That is because his defensive principles are the very foundations of today's defense-oriented centers. He might even be more versatile than most of the shot-blockers that played in the 80s and 90s. And considering that Russell could obviously contain a much bigger Wilt Chamberlain in their battles, size was not a factor that would hinder Bill in the modern-day NBA.

As Red said, a more refined offensive player like Hakeem Olajuwon (considered to be the most skillful center in league history) might have given Bill Russell some trouble.[xii] Sure, with how much bigger and more athletic today's players are, Bill might not have blocked as many shots in today's NBA. However, because Russell was always studying opponent tendencies and learning new ways of defending them, he would have figured out guys like Olajuwon, O'Neal, Robinson, Embiid, and Davis.

With all that considered, Bill Russell is still the single greatest defensive force in the NBA and has contributed significantly to how teams and players play defense in today's modern-day league. And because of how his defense was able to translate to 11 championship rings for the Boston Celtics, he truly gives justice to the saying, "Offense wins games, but defense wins championships."

Russell has also made a significant impact outside of the basketball court, but still within the confines of the sport. He was the first African-American to be named a head coach, not only in the NBA but also in all of America's major sporting leagues. He also broke down social barriers and paved the way for African-Americans or people from different racial and ethnic backgrounds to find success as coaches or even as executives of different teams and organizations all across America.

Nowadays, it is not very surprising to see that there are more black head coaches than there are white coaches. Thanks to Bill Russell, the NBA has learned not to see people of color but to only see aptitude. It no longer matters whether you are black or white, African or American, Muslim, or Christian, as long as you can excel at what you do.

The great ones not only leave a lasting impact on the way the game is being played but also on the way it is being handled off the basketball court. In that regard, Bill Russell has done great things for basketball both as a pioneer defender and trailblazing head coach. You would be hard-pressed to find anyone who has had that same impact on basketball.

Chapter 7: Legacy

Not a lot of players in the history of this great sport can match the accomplishments that Bill Russell compiled in the 13 seasons he played in the NBA. Because of that, he has left a legacy of greatness that probably no other player past, present, or future can even come close to matching or achieving.

When you hear Bill Russell's name, you will most likely equate it to winning. After all, the man won 11 NBA championships over a span of 13 seasons. He did so on multiple occasions, both as a player and as a head coach. In doing so, he was able to collect five MVP awards even though he was usually up against players that could put up better stats and higher scoring numbers. And on top of that, he won the NCAA championship twice in a row and also won an Olympic gold medal.

Given that, it is not difficult to say that Bill Russell ranks as one of the most decorated athletes not only in basketball but also in the entire world of sports. His legacy is one that is built on excellence, and he became the standard for what it means to be great not only in basketball or sports but in all other kinds of competitive endeavors as well. Whether it is in music, academics, politics, or finances, one cannot truly call himself the greatest if he has not come close to what Bill Russell did.

While some players have tried to come close, they ultimately fall short in reaching the heights of greatness that Bill Russell has achieved. Kareem Abdul-Jabbar won six championships and six MVP awards. Magic Johnson is a five-time champion and three-time MVP. Of course, Michael Jordan is a six-time champion and five-time MVP. No matter whose name you throw into the conversation, they will always fall short of the 11 championships and five MVP awards that Russell achieved in his career.

Yes, individually, there are players that are far better than Russell. Michael Jordan is considered one of the greatest of all time, not only because of his achievements but also because of how great of a player he was on the court. Some say that LeBron James is not far behind Jordan in that regard. To some extent, there are those that would say that Kareem Abdul-Jabbar, Hakeem Olajuwon, and Shaquille O'Neal are all better centers than Bill Russell. However, people often forget that Russell was still as great as anyone at the individual level.

When looking at Russell's career rebounding average of 22.5 (second overall) and total career rebounds of 21,620 (second overall), one cannot disregard how truly talented an individual player he was, especially on rebounding and defense. He is also only one of two players to have 50 or more rebounds in a single game. And had they been counting blocks as official stats back in the '60s, there is no doubt that Russell would rank high on the list.

Bill Russell's numbers might seem inflated, especially if you consider the pace of the game and how many more shots they were missing back then, but you still cannot discount him as one of the greatest individual players in league history. Being one of the best rebounders and shot-blockers the game has ever seen is still part of the legacy of greatness that Bill Russell holds to this day. And when you add that up to his overall individual and team accomplishments, you might even think of him as the greatest of all time.

The NBA also recognizes Russell as one of the true greats that the sport has ever seen. After Bill Russell's death in 2022, the NBA and NBPA announced that his No. 6 jersey would be retired across the entire league. No one would be allowed to use the number ever again, with the exception of the players that wore the No. 6 jersey before the NBA decided to retire it.[xviii]

"It was always a treat seeing him at games, having an opportunity to win championships, see him up on the panel and give me the Bill Russell Award was one of the most delightful moments of my career," said LeBron James, one of the last few people allowed to wear the No. 6 jersey.

In that regard, Russell's greatness as a winner was one that the entire league felt because his passing left a huge hole in the heart of the entire NBA. He was not only a pioneer that helped revolutionize the defensive aspect of the sport but was also one of the names that actively fought for the rights of people of color in the entire country. The fact that Russell was not only a great winner but was also a civil rights activist was one of the things that made him a generational personality in any professional sport. And while he may not have had the same kind of opportunities that the players of today's generation were able to enjoy, Bill Russell's power as a star was one that the entire league respected and revered.

So, with all that said, is Bill Russell the greatest player of all time? That is a debate that remains unsettled, especially considering that there are a lot of players that can lay claim to that distinction.

But is Bill Russell the greatest *winner* of all time? Without question, the answer is a resounding YES.

Final Word/About the Author

I was born and raised in Norwalk, Connecticut. Growing up, I could often be found spending many nights watching basketball, soccer, and football matches with my father in the family living room. I love sports and everything that sports can embody. I believe that sports are one of the most genuine forms of competition, heart, and determination. I write my works to learn more about influential athletes in the hopes that from my writing, you the reader can walk away inspired to put in an equal if not greater amount of hard work and perseverance to pursue your goals. If you enjoyed *Bill Russell: The Inspiring Story of One of Basketball's Legendary Centers,* please leave a review! Also, you can read more of my works on *David Ortiz, Cody Bellinger, Alex Bregman, Francisco Lindor, Shohei Ohtani, Ronald Acuna Jr., Javier Baez, Jose Altuve, Christian Yelich, Max Scherzer, Mookie Betts, Pete Alonso, Clayton Kershaw, Mike Trout, Bryce Harper, Jackie Robinson, Justin Verlander, Derek Jeter, Ichiro Suzuki, Ken Griffey Jr., Babe Ruth, Aaron Judge, Novak Djokovic, Roger Federer, Rafael Nadal, Serena Williams, Naomi Osaka, Coco Gauff, Baker Mayfield, George Kittle, Matt Ryan, Matthew Stafford, Eli Manning, Khalil Mack, Davante Adams, Terry Bradshaw, Jimmy Garoppolo, Philip Rivers, Von Miller, Aaron Donald, Joey Bosa, Josh Allen, Mike Evans, Joe Burrow, Carson Wentz Adam Thielen, Stefon Diggs, Lamar Jackson, Dak Prescott, Patrick Mahomes, Odell Beckham Jr., J.J. Watt, Colin Kaepernick, Aaron Rodgers, Tom Brady, Russell Wilson, Peyton Manning, Drew Brees, Calvin Johnson, Brett Favre, Rob Gronkowski, Andrew Luck, Richard Sherman, Bill Belichick, Candace Parker, Skylar Diggins-Smith, A'ja Wilson, Lisa Leslie, Sue Bird, Diana Taurasi, Julius Erving, Clyde Drexler, John Havlicek, Oscar Robertson, Ja Morant, Gary Payton, Khris Middleton, Michael Porter*

Jr., Julius Randle, Jrue Holiday, Domantas Sabonis, Mike Conley Jr., Jerry West, Dikembe Mutombo, Fred VanVleet, Jamal Murray, Zion Williamson, Brandon Ingram, Jaylen Brown, Charles Barkley, Trae Young, Andre Drummond, JJ Redick, DeMarcus Cousins, Wilt Chamberlain, Bradley Beal, Rudy Gobert, Aaron Gordon, Kristaps Porzingis, Nikola Vucevic, Andre Iguodala, Devin Booker, John Stockton, Jeremy Lin, Chris Paul, Pascal Siakam, Jayson Tatum, Gordon Hayward, Nikola Jokic, Victor Oladipo, Luka Doncic, Ben Simmons, Shaquille O'Neal, Joel Embiid, Donovan Mitchell, Damian Lillard, Giannis Antetokounmpo, Chris Bosh, Kemba Walker, Isaiah Thomas, DeMar DeRozan, Amar'e Stoudemire, Al Horford, Yao Ming, Marc Gasol, Draymond Green, Kawhi Leonard, Dwyane Wade, Ray Allen, Pau Gasol, Dirk Nowitzki, Jimmy Butler, Paul Pierce, Manu Ginobili, Pete Maravich, Larry Bird, Kyle Lowry, Jason Kidd, David Robinson, LaMarcus Aldridge, Derrick Rose, Paul George, Kevin Garnett, Michael Jordan, LeBron James, Kyrie Irving, Klay Thompson, Stephen Curry, Kevin Durant, Russell Westbrook, Chris Paul, Blake Griffin, Kobe Bryant, Anthony Davis, Joakim Noah, Scottie Pippen, Carmelo Anthony, Kevin Love, Grant Hill, Tracy McGrady, Vince Carter, Patrick Ewing, Karl Malone, Tony Parker, Allen Iverson, Hakeem Olajuwon, Reggie Miller, Michael Carter-Williams, James Harden, John Wall, Tim Duncan, Steve Nash, Gregg Popovich, Pat Riley, John Wooden, Steve Kerr, Brad Stevens, Red Auerbach, Doc Rivers, Erik Spoelstra, Mike D'Antoni, and *Phil Jackson* in the Kindle Store. If you love basketball, check out my website at claytongeoffreys.com to join my exclusive list where I let you know about my latest books and give you lots of goodies.

Like what you read? Please leave a review!

I write because I love sharing the stories of influential athletes like Bill Russell with fantastic readers like you. My readers inspire me to write more so please do not hesitate to let me know what you thought by leaving a review! If you love books on life, basketball, or productivity, check out my website at claytongeoffreys.com to join my exclusive list where I let you know about my latest books. Aside from being the first to hear about my latest releases, you can also download a free copy of *33 Life Lessons: Success Principles, Career Advice & Habits of Successful People*. See you there!

Clayton

References

[i] "Bill Russell". *NBA.com*. Web.

[ii] Graham. "The Man Behind the Rings: The Story of Bill Russell Pt.1". *Bleacher Report*. 31 July 2009. Web.

[iii] Thompson, Tim. "Bill Russell overcome long odds, dominated basketball". *The Current (University of Missouri-St. Louis)*.

[iv] Taylor, John (2005). *The Rivalry: Bill Russell, Wilt Chamberlain, and the Golden Age of Basketball*. New York City: Random House.

[v] "Chat Transcript: Celtics Legend Bill Russell". *NBA.com*. Web.

[vi] Sven, Simon (December 2007). "Wir sind stolz auf Dirk" [We are proud of Dirk]. *Five*.

[vii] Russell, Bill. *Red and Me: My Coach, My Lifelong Friend*. HarperCollins.

[viii] "A conversation with Bill Russell". *USAtoday.com*. 21 January 2005. Web.

[ix] Schneider, Bernie. "1953-56 NCAA Championship Seasons: The Bill Russell Years". *USFDons.com*. 2006. Web.

[x] "Interview: Bill Russell—Cornerstone of the Boston Celtics' Dynasty". *Academy of Achievement*. 4 July 2008. Web.

[xi] Terrell, Roy. "The Tournament and the Man Who". *Sports Illustrated*. 1 January 1956. Web.

[xii] "Russell of Celtics Violates N.B.A. Rules on Defense, Coach of Warriors Says". *The New York Times*. January 3, 1957.

[xiii] Walker, Sam. "The 'Coleman Play' introduced—and defined—Bill Russell's never-say-die leadership to Boston". *Boston*. 4 June 2017. Web.

[xiv] Ryan, Bob. "Timeless Excellence". *NBA.com*. Web.

[xv] Russell, Bill (5 May 2009). *Red and Me: My Coach, My Lifelong Friend*. HarperCollins.

[xvi] MacMullan, Jackie. "Jordan, Russell, Kareem, even the King of Pop—the astonishing mentors who shaped Kobe Bryant". *ESPN*. 5 April 2020. Web.

[xvii] Himmelsbach, Adam. "Why was Boston Garden nearly empty when Bill Russell's number was retired in 1972?". *Boston Globe*. 7 October 2017. Web.

[xviii] "Bill Russell's No. 6 jersey to be retired throughout NBA." *NBA.com*. Web.

Made in United States
North Haven, CT
10 August 2023

40174479R00061